VOICES

Native American Hymns and Worship Resources

The Native American Hymnal and
Worship Resource Committee

D'ISCIPLESHIP RESOURCES

P.O. BOX 340003 • NASHVILLE, TN 37203-0003
www.discipleshipresources.org

Art work:

Cover design by Z. Susanne Aikman (Eastern Cherokee)
© 1992

The drawings on pages 1, 37, 63, and 85, and the border
designs on the title page and pages 1, 13, 35, 53, 61, and
82 are by Carolyn Risling Shaw (Karuk-Yurok-Hupa,
Northern California coast). Used by permission.

The texts that appear with the drawings on pages 1, 37,
63, and 85 are from "Friends Can Be Good Medicine,"
Shenandoah Films (Arcata, California), and are used by
permission of the California Department of Mental Health.

The texts that appear in Cherokee alphabet on pages 15,
18, and 19 are from *Cherokee Hymns,* Nos. 26, 36, and
87 (Indian Heritage Association: Fayetteville, Arkansas
72701).

Reprinted 2000
ISBN 0-88177-095-7

DR095

Contents

WORSHIP RESOURCES

CALLS TO WORSHIP

PRAYERS OF CONFESSION

OTHER PRAYERS

OTHER RESOURCES

INDEXES

Acknowledgments

For many years various individuals and groups have expressed the need for a Native American hymnal—a collection of hymns and other worship resources that would represent the various languages, customs, and cultural traditions of Native American Christianity. The collection of material for this volume began in July 1988.

It would be impossible to thank every person individually who has contributed to the development of this collection. In addition to the individuals whose names appear in the credit lines of the pages which follow, we owe a debt of gratitude to many others whose gifts of time and talent have gone unnamed—those who were not authors or composers but helped to identify and locate the materials that should be included; those who translated and paraphrased the words from their languages into English so others could gain insight; those who shared their music, sometimes over the telephone; those who transcribed the music, so the living treasure of the oral tradition could at least be glimpsed in print; those who spent many hours verifying sources and seeking permissions—all of these deserve our heartfelt thanks for a job well done.

In addition, I would like to recognize a number of organizations whose support has been instrumental in bringing these resources to print. The Native American International Caucus and the Oklahoma Indian Missionary Conference have played a key role throughout. In the early stages, they recognized the need for this resource, and called for the establishment of the Native American Hymnal/Worship Resource Committee which, in turn, accepted the challenge of launching the entire effort and supported the Project Director as the basic manuscript was created. Support for publication of the manuscript came through The General Board of Discipleship of The United Methodist Church—specifically, the Section on Worship, the Section on Ethnic Local Church Concerns, and Discipleship Resources, the publishing unit—all of whom saw the vision for and recognized the value of what you now hold in your hands. A special word of appreciation goes to Gamut Music Productions whose skill in book design and typesetting is evident on every page.

The greatest debt of gratitude, however, is owed to those countless individuals and groups of Native American Christians who have been willing to share their songs, prayers, and stories of faith so the worship of others might be enriched. From them these resources have been received. To them this collection is dedicated. May it serve in some small way to extend the circle of sharing ever wider.

Marilyn M. Hofstra (Choctaw, Chickasaw), Project Director
Native American Hymnal/Worship Resource
Arcata, California
January 1992

Preface

The publication of a collection of Native American hymns and worship resources raises a basic question: Can one respect and preserve one's own cultural traditions and still be a good Christian? This is a question that Native Americans have always had to face in becoming Christian. Their answers echo in the "voices" which fill the pages of this volume.

Native American culture itself is many-sided. There are between 250 and 400 language groups of Native Americans indigenous to the North American continent, depending upon how one defines the groups. Traditions and cultures vary widely, as do languages and meanings of similar-sounding words.

For all the differences among the nations, tribes, clans, and families of Native Americans, however, some things are nearly universal. One is a concern for the well-being of the family-clan-tribe-nation itself. The idea of "love one another" was not entirely new to Native Americans when the first Christian missionaries arrived a few short centuries ago. Likewise, "Indians" are an oral people. Our traditions and wisdom are passed from one generation to the next in spoken word. Our worship has been shared in spoken and sung prayer since the grass was new upon Mother Earth.

Thus, the Apostle Paul was not the first to urge people to "pray without ceasing." Native Americans have traditions which stress that because life is a gift from God, everything one does with life is a gift back to God and, thus, a communication with God. Speaking and singing in ceremonial settings, such as Christian worship, are very pointedly communicating with God. But even love songs and songs full of humor are prayer. Because the Creator formed human beings to feel the emotions which accompany the songs, and because all of life is a prayer, so too is music. Such has been the belief among Native Americans since the oral traditions began thousands of years ago.

Unfortunately, the introduction of Christianity to North America was marked all too often by efforts on the part of missionaries to require Native Americans to adopt styles of worship once current in Europe. It is amusing to some of our elders today to see the "new" form of worship called "liturgical dance." Indians were once told by Christian missionaries that it was improper to dance in worship. Somehow, too, it was improper to worship God in one's own mother-tongue, as though God were limited to understanding only Spanish, Latin, German, French, or English. It was further unacceptable to worship in songs that made sense to one's own heart, speaking about ways of living with which one was familiar. Instead, proper songs apparently needed to be culturally incomprehensible, perhaps to make more poignant the leap of faith required to accept them as an expression of a new Christian's heart-feelings.

The Christian missionaries who went among the Native Americans had, for the most part, the best of intentions. They had a goal with which all who are Christians can sympathize. They wanted to take Christ to the Indians. Many of the missionaries, however, had a difficulty. Quite simply, they were not able to distinguish between the power or presence of Christ and the European cultural soil in which their own faith had first taken root. Native Americans lived differently and had, for the most part, no written language. Europeans were primarily a written-language people and tended to judge the degree of civilization and the religious capacity of other peoples by this standard. It did not occur to them that people could be highly intelligent, "civilized," open to God and, indeed, ready to follow Christ, with an oral-language-based culture.

Native Americans thought, and in some instances still think, that Europeans were a deprived people because they lacked the chain of person-to-person linkage—the linkage of present to past and future that comes through the very personal vehicle of spoken and sung history and shared worship forms. So, now, it is amusing to some elders to find that church growth experts are encouraging churches to become more interpersonal in order to keep people involved. We have a saying: What goes around comes around. And, it looks as though it has.

Can one respect and preserve one's own cultural traditions and still be a good Christian? In this book you will find the answer of those who have spent so much of themselves in preparing it. As you study the bits of wisdom, the sayings of the elders, and the rhythm of native words for traditional Christian hymns, it is hoped that you will find a new appreciation for the way in which different cultural traditions can complement each other and create a helpful, guiding, healing, inspiring, saving, and graceful tool for enhancing the Christian worship of God.

In this light, the resources of this collection offer a new opportunity for all of us to be open to the presence and power of Christ as he meets us in the earthen/cultural vessels of our worship traditions. For those who are not Native American, here is an opportunity to touch the linkage of living history and feeling that Native Americans share in their view of the world and in their relationship with God through Jesus Christ. For those who are Native American, here is a place where people of all tribes and nations can find a common ground, in written sounds gathered from the four directions. There are precious few such resources available.

The logo on the cover is symbolic in many ways. Designed by United Methodist artist Z. Susanne Aikman (Eastern Cherokee), the center of the design is the cross. As it happens, this design also reflects a number of familiar Native American symbols. The central point of two roads going in opposite directions speaks of the centered life—harmony, balance, or, as the Navajo say, beauty. The four points of the compass are the sacred four directions. Each quadrant of the design, moreover, contains patterns that reflect Native American cultures in different regions of the continent. Above all, the logo portrays the coming together of many traditions in one symbol of unity.

Voices is not definitive of all Native American hymnody, either traditional or Christian. Such would not be a book, but a library. Most of the materials in this collection, indeed, were gathered with the help of Native American Christians affiliated with The United Methodist Church. In all, about two dozen different tribal groups across the continent are represented. Even this limited sample, however, can convey the spirit and purpose of the work you have before you.

If *Voices* succeeds at all, it will be because it is near the centerpoint of the cover logo, where the roads of various traditions intersect. Though no national or tribal group may say it encapsulates their entire tradition, it is hoped that all can say, "Yes, this feels familiar."

If this concept of trying to present something familiar to enhance worship still draws a raised eyebrow, it is good to remember that it has an esteemed tradition. After all, John and Charles Wesley, founders of Methodism, in order to help the unlettered of their day to sing God's praises, set the words of their hymns to popular tavern songs. The Wesleyan message was for people who literally were often not allowed to enter a church, and many of whom could not have read the prayer book once inside. Somehow it seems right that the oral tradition of Native Americans be lifted up in a United Methodist book because of the great reliance on oral presentation of the faith by the Wesleys.

Look again at the cover logo: Christ is the center. John Wesley came to this continent to convert the Indians and bring them to Christ. He failed miserably, most likely because he wanted Indians to act like Englishmen. But what if John Wesley had done for the Native Americans what he did for the coal miners? What wonders of conversion could he have wrought had he set his brother's "Oh For a Thousand Tongues to Sing" to the sixty-four count rhythm of a powwow love song, a tune recognizable and singable within the tradition of the potential converts?

Voices: Native American Hymns and Worship Resources is a written version of parts of our Native American oral tradition because we want our sisters and brothers to understand that Christ is the center. It is that simple.

D. Donald Donato (Cherokee, Choctaw)
Rocky Mountain Annual Conference
The United Methodist Church
January 1992

Introduction

PURPOSE OF THE COLLECTION

Voices: Native American Hymns and Worship Resources has been compiled and arranged with a specific purpose in view. This purpose is to enable Native Americans of various nations and tribes to share their traditions of worship with one another, and with non-Native Americans as well. As simple as the purpose sounds in itself, however, the way forward toward achieving it has been anything but simple.

The basic task in compiling the collection was to gather hymns and worship resources from a wide variety of Native American groups. To be sure, Native American hymn books had been published before, but these were usually in the language and tradition of only one tribe—for example, the *Cherokee Hymn Book* (Indian Heritage Association) and Muskokee Hymns (Presbyterian Board of Christian Education). The goal for *Voices*, by contrast, was to gather hymns in the original languages of several tribes, and to gather worship resources in English translation or composition. The desire was that the hymns could be taught in the original languages to culturally diverse congregations, and worship resources could be shared in what would be for many a common tongue.

ORGANIZATION OF THE COLLECTION

The results of this gathering process are now visible in the Table of Contents. Hymns are listed alphabetically according to their common titles—the titles by which they are known in the various Native American traditions. Thus, the title of a hymn may be either in a native language (e.g., "Cesvs Purke Likan," Muscogee-Creek, page 12), or a reference to the title as it appears in another hymn book (e.g., "Cherokee Hymn 87: Christ's Second Coming," page 4), or simply the name of another well-known English hymn whose tune or text has been adapted by a particular tribe (e.g., the "Caddo" words to the tune of "Amazing Grace," page 6).

Apart from the adapted English hymns, few resources are available today that provide the musical notation for many of these songs. The style of notation is intentionally simple. Even an inexperienced musician can learn and use it. Some who have sung these songs for years may feel that the music is "a little different from the way I sing it." For the most part, however, this is due simply to differences of personal or regional styling.

The "Worship Resources" of the collection, on the other hand, are grouped according to liturgical functions—e.g., "calls to worship," "prayers of confession" —and then listed alphabetically by common titles within these groupings. Whenever possible, the national or tribal source of each selection is listed along with the title.

Taken together, the hymns and worship resources display a significant range of theological emphasis. This will perhaps come as no surprise in view of the variety of national and tribal sources involved. The collection is not arranged theologically, yet certain centers of thematic gravity can be discerned. Among the hymns, for example, the themes of "Jesus' love," "heaven," and "eternal life" are prominent. Something similar can be said with respect to the themes of "nature" and "creation" in the worship resources. All such thematic emphases may be perused in more detail in the Index of Topics and Categories beginning on page 91.

SOURCES OF THE COLLECTION

Regrettably, it has not been possible to represent each of the 250 to 400 language groups of Native Americans that Don Donato mentions in his Preface. In fact, taking into account all of the contributions, it has only been possible to include material from about twenty different national or tribal groups. A complete list of the selections included from each nation or tribe is provided in the Index of Native American Nations and Tribes beginning on page 88.

Every effort has been made to trace the original national and tribal source of each selection, and to give proper credit to all individual contributors—authors, composers, arrangers, translators, etc. In many cases, however, it has not been possible to trace the complete lineage. There is no doubt that individual Native American authors and composers were involved in the creation of hymns currently identified simply by reference to the tribal tradition. The names of these individuals, however, have not always been handed down with the tradition.

Likewise, individual arrangers, translators, and transcribers were surely involved in creating and handing along the native words and/or tunes that have now been adapted to such well-known English hymns as "Come, Thou Fount of Every Blessing" (page 20), "Jesus Loves Me" (page 40), and "Praise God, from Whom All Blessings Flow" (page 46). To the trained ear, moreover, some of the "traditional" Native American hymns may also suggest lines of development stretching back to other European and African American sources. In keeping with the spontaneity and adaptability of oral traditions, however, these lines of development have often gone unrecorded.

The credits which appear with each selection represent the best information that the compilers and editors have been able to obtain through a lengthy process of inquiry and investigation. They will be grateful for any additional information that readers and users may be able to supply.

SPECIAL FEATURES OF THE COLLECTION

Distinct from but not unrelated to the difficulty of identifying sources, the editorial committee of *Voices* had to face a second major challenge—the challenge of linguistic diversity, both in the spoken and in the written word. It is one thing to imagine a worship setting where members of various tribes share their traditions with one another, and with non-Native Americans, by means of the spoken word. In this setting learners hear the words of a hymn sounded out, and learn, as we say, "by ear." It is quite another matter, however, to create a literary resource that conveys all of the necessary information by means of the printed page alone.

The basic challenge in this regard has been to discover a uniform means of spelling and pronunciation for the various Native American languages involved.

What may need to be emphasized in this regard is that Native Americans not only belong to different nations and tribes, and speak different languages; they also use different forms of written communication in order to convey the sounds of their languages in print—different alphabets, syllabaries, and pronouncing guides. Some tribes have developed their own alphabets—see, for example, the Cherokee texts on pages 15, 18, and 19. Others have adapted the Arabic alphabet—for example the Muscogee and the Kiowa texts on pages 5, 8, and elsewhere.

Even when the same alphabet has been adopted, however, criteria for the transposition of sounds into letters can vary considerably from region to region, even within the circle of one nation. The sound represented by "ee" in one phonetic spelling might be represented in another by "ei," and in yet another by an alphabetic symbol unique to the writing of only one tribe. Unless such variations are addressed, it could be very difficult, if not impossible, for a variety of worship leaders and worshipers to determine how the words of a particular Native American text should sound when sung.

With this in mind, the compilers and editors of *Voices* accepted the challenge of providing a system of "common phonetic transliteration" for as many hymn texts as possible. The process of producing a common phonetic transliteration involves transposing ("transliterating") the alphabetic symbols of one spelling system into a more widely recognizable ("common") and easily pronounced ("phonetic") spelling. These alternate spellings, and the Guide to Pronunciation beginning on page 86 to which they are related, are simply an attempt to recognize the most significant differences among the written languages, and to provide help in pronouncing some of the more difficult letter combinations. In addition to knowing the meaning of each hymn through translation or paraphrase, then, persons of varying tribal and cultural backgrounds will also be able to pronounce the basic sounds of the original languages.

Notice, this moves *Voices* beyond the role of simply translating the meaning of hymns into a common tongue. Most of the hymns in this collection include an English translation or paraphrase. But these versions are not, for the most part, intended to be sung; nor in most cases can they be.

Following this system a typical hymn entry will appear in one of two formats. When a Native American hymn is identified with the tradition of only one nation or tribe (see, for example, "Seneca Hymn 152," page 52), the format of the hymn will include the following elements: 1) common phonetic transliteration interlined in the music, 2) original Native American text immediately following the music (preserving unique alphabetic characters or distinctive uses of the Arabic alphabet), and 3) an English translation or paraphrase. (The term *translation* is used only in those cases where the English version follows the poetic form of the original Native American text—line for line, meter for meter.)

A different format has been required when a familiar English hymn tune provides a common starting point for the hymn texts of several different Native American nations or tribes (see, for example, "Amazing Grace," beginning on page 6). In this case, the format of the hymn will include the following elements: 1) English words interlined in the music, 2) original Native American texts (usually in common phonetic transliteration), and 3) additional English translations or paraphrases where they are needed.

Despite efforts to remain consistent with these formats, a number of variations have been unavoidable. Several such variations should be noted among the "adapted" English hymns. In some cases, for example, it was not possible, given limited time and resources, to acquire the desired common phonetic transliteration for each of the Native American texts (see the Muscogee-Creek text for "Amazing Grace," page 8). In such cases, unfortunately, worshipers may stumble over the pronunciation unless someone is present who can read and pronounce the Native American language in question.

Likewise, readers and worshipers may notice some variations in the way English translations or paraphrases are provided. Some of the Native American texts that appear with "Amazing Grace," for example, are translated; others are not. The principle that was pursued in this regard was simple: Translate only those Native American texts that depart significantly from the meaning of the original English version. Thus, the Choctaw text of "Amazing Grace"—which speaks at length about the role of the Holy Spirit—is translated; the Caddo text is not. It was not possible to acquire a translation of the Cheyenne text, however, even though it too clearly departs from the original with the appearance of Jesus' name in the first line.

Beyond these kinds of variations, a few other matters may be a source of some confusion or doubt to users of this volume, especially those not previously familiar with the ways of oral tradition. A question may arise, for example, as to why the Native American words of a particular text appear in more than one place (see, for example, the words to "Cherokee Hymn 87: Christ's Second Coming," pages 4, 7, and 18; or the words to "Choctaw Hymn 48," pages 4 and 7). Similarly, the English words to Isaac Watts' composition, "Alas! and Did My Savior Bleed," appear in two places (pages 2 and 32). Closer investigation of these hymns will reveal, however, that in each case something has changed—either the tune to which the text is set, or some part of the text itself. Such repetitions might appear strange in some hymnals. In *Voices,* they are a natural reflection of the spontaneity, flexibility, and adaptability that characterize the oral traditions of Native America.

CONCLUSION

Singers and worshipers should look to find in this collection not one monolithic Native American tradition, but the signs of many traditions—centered on Christ, yet changing, modulating, and being shared in different ways. Such traditions are not easy to represent in the fixed medium of print. In some ways the standards that normally guide the publication of a "hymnal" have guided *Voices* as well. In other ways, these standards have had to be overruled precisely in order to allow *Voices* to set its own standard. As the members of different Native American groups and non-Native Americans share these resources, the witness of *Voices* will be heard. In this way, *Voices* will do more to blaze a trail than simply to follow one.

Hymns

Our traditions. . .
Where we turn and return for wisdom and strength,
to renew our spiritual ties to each other,
and to the land.

Alas! and Did My Savior Bleed

1. A - las! and did my Sav - ior bleed, and did my Sov - ereign die? Would he de - vote that sa - cred head for sin - ners such as I?
2. Was it for crimes that I have done, he groaned up - on the tree? A - maz - ing pit - y! Grace un - known! And love be - yond de - gree!
3. Well might the sun in dark - ness hide, and shut its glo - ries in, when God, the might - y mak - er, died for his own crea - ture's sin.
4. Thus might I hide my blush - ing face while his dear cross ap - pears; dis - solve my heart in thank - ful - ness, and melt mine eyes to tears.
5. But drops of tears can ne'er re - pay the debt of love I owe. Here, Lord, I give my - self a - way; 'tis all that I can do.

WORDS: Isaac Watts; refrain by Ralph E. Hudson
MUSIC: Anon.; arr. by Ralph E. Hudson

Refrain

At the cross, at the cross, where I first saw the light, and the bur-den of my heart rolled a - way; it was there by faith I re - ceived my sight, and now I am hap-py all the day.

Cherokee Hymn 87: Christ's Second Coming

Cherokee:

1. Oo-neh-lah-nuh-hee Oo-weh-jee
Ee-gah-goo-yuh-heh-ee,
hnah-qwo jo-suh wee-oo-lo-seh
Ee-gah-goo-yuh-ho-nuh.

Refrain

Oo jah tee yoo wo doo nah nee wey
nah nah nee
Ee gah do juh loo sah doo jo suh yee
Gey nah nee wee gah nah nah noo go
goo
Joo wah doo hee do dee dah nel loo.

2. Ee-seh-no ee-oo-neh-jeh-ee
Ah-yoo-no doo-leh-nuh,
Tah-lee-neh duh-jee-loo-jee-lee,
Oo-duh-neh oo-neh-juh.

3. Eh-lah-nee-guh duh-lee-sqwah-dee
Gah-loo-juh-hah Ee-yoo;
Nee-gah-dee dah-yeh-dee-go-ee
Ah-nee eh-lah-nee-guh.

4. Oo-nah-dah-nuh-tee ah-neh-huh
Do-duh-yah-nuh-hee-lee,
Jo-suh hnah-qwo nee-go-hee-luh
Do-hee wah-neh-hee-sdee.

English paraphrase:

Jesus, Son of God, paid the price for us and now he has gone on to heaven. But he said as he departed, "I will come again the second time." We will all see him when he comes back to this earth again to claim his own.

Refrain

There is unending singing that rings throughout all the many mansions. There is light always.

WORDS: Stanzas from the *Cherokee Hymn Book*; refrain anon.; common phonetic transliteration by Marilyn M. Hofstra (Choctaw, Chickasaw) © 1992; Eng. paraphrase by Jennie Lee Fife (Cherokee) © 1992

Choctaw Hymn 48

Choctaw:

1. Shee-lom-bish Ho-lee-to-pah mah!
Ish meen-tee pol-lah chah,
Hah-tahk eel-buh-shah pee-ah hah
Ish pee yok-pah-lah-shkee.

2. Pee chok-osh no-see ah-tok-mah
Ahnt ish ok-chuh-lah-shkee,
Ish pee yo-bee-ee-cheek-bah-no;
Ee cheem ah-uh-neh-shkee.

3. Shee-lom-bish Ho-lee-to-pah mah!
Peem ah-nok-fee-lah huht
Ok-theel-it kuh-nee-uh ho-kah,
Ish pee on to-mah-shkee.

English paraphrase:

1. Come, O Holy Spirit!
Come to us who are poor in spirit.
Bless us!

2. Come and awaken our hearts.
Give us your peace,
we implore you.

3. O Holy Spirit!
Our minds are clothed in darkness.
Enlighten us!

4. Pee chok-ush nok-hahk-lo yo-kah
   Ahnt pee ho-po-luh-chee:
   Eel ah-uh-shuh-chee-kah yo-kah,
   Ish pee kah-sho-fah-shkee.

4. Our hearts are filled with sorrow.
   Come and comfort us, sinners that
   we are.
   Cleanse us!

WORDS: Trad. Choctaw; common phonetic transliteration by Marilyn M. Hofstra (Choctaw, Chickasaw)
© 1992; Eng. paraphrase by Harry Folsom (Choctaw) © 1992

Muscogee Hymn 32

Muscogee (Creek):

1. Ahee-huh! Kuht! chuh Hee-sah-yee
      juh
   Chah-tah puhl-loht-kuht hahks?
   Moh-men uhm Meek-ko ee-luht
      hahks?
   Chune-tuh yo-moo-see-yahn?

Refrain

At the cross, ...

2. Uhn-ee hol-wah-yee-chi-yah-ten
   Ee-toh uh-tuhlth-kuht hahks?
   Es-toh-mah-hee uh-no-keech-kuh
   Mon-tah-loht sah-see-kos!

3. Huh-see mo-muh-thlee tee-tah-yen
   Yo-mooch-ket o-muh-tees,
   Hee-sah-kee-tuh-mee-see ee-lof
   Est'en hol-wah-yeech-kuhn!

4. Toh-weck-lehp-kuhnhee-chi-yo-
      fuht,
   Chuh toh-thlo-fuh ee-heht
   Uhl-soo-sen: chuh fee-kee kaf-ken;
   Es huh-kay-ki-yeht os.

5. Chuh tuhlth-o-poos-wuh puh-laht-
      kees,
   Uhm uh-hoo-thlee fee-kehks;
   Toh-kuhs! Mo-juh chem ee way-
      kees!
   Ee-tuh es-toh-muh-kos.

English paraphrase:

*Stanzas 1, 2, and 3, and the refrain,
have basically the same meaning as in
the original English (see page 2).*

4. When I see the cross, I hide my face
   in shame. I cry/weep, my heart
   grieves.

5. My tears fall, my debt was paid.
   Now, I'm ready to surrender; I can
   do nothing else.

WORDS: *Muskokee Hymns*, Hymn 32; common phonetic transliteration and Eng. paraphrase by Leona Sullivan (Creek) © 1992

Amazing Grace

1. A - maz - ing grace! How sweet the sound that saved a wretch like me! I once was lost, but now am found; was blind, but now I see.
2. 'Twas grace that taught my heart to fear, and grace my fears re - lieved; how pre - cious did that grace ap - pear the hour I first be - lieved.
3. Through man - y dan - gers, toils, and snares, I have al - read - y come; 'tis grace hath brought me safe thus far, and grace will lead me home.
4. The Lord has prom - ised good to me, his word my hope se - cures; he will my shield and por - tion be, as long as life en - dures.
5. Yea, when this flesh and heart shall fail, and mor - tal life shall cease, I shall pos - sess with- in the veil, a life of joy and peace.
6. When we've been there ten thou - sand years, bright shin - ing as the sun, we've no less days to sing God's praise than when we first be - gun.

WORDS: John Newton; st. 6 anon.;
MUSIC: 19th cent. USA melody; harm. by Edwin O. Excell

Caddo

Dah-newn bah-'we-aht, Ah-ah ha-you
He-E-k'ay is-dud, dah-ah
Se tah-yah o-e-ah
Ha-bah-lah ku-hay-yah
Nah-dah-new tahn chay-bah.

WORDS: Trad. Caddo

Cherokee Hymn 87: Christ's Second Coming

Cherokee:

1. Oo-neh-lah-nuh-hee oo-weh-jee
   Ee-gah-goo-yuh-hee-ee,
   hnah-qwo jo-suh wee-oo-lo-seh
   Ee-gah-goo-yuh-ho-nah.

2. Ee-seh-no ee-oo-neh-jeh-ee
   Ah-yoo-no doo-leh-nuh,
   Tah-lee-neh duh-jee-loo-jee-lee,
   Oo-duh-neh-oo-neh-juh.

3. Eh-lah-nee-guh duh-lee-sqwah-dee
   Gah-loo-juh-hah Ee-yoo;
   Nee-gah-dee dah-yeh-dee-go-ee
   Ah-nee eh-lah-nee-guh.

4. Oo-nah-dah-nuh tee ah-neh-huh
   Do-duh-yah-nuh-hee-lee,
   Jo-eh hnah-qwo nee-go-hee-luh
   Do-hee wah-neh-heh-sdee.

English paraphrase:

Jesus, Son of God, paid the price for us and now he has gone on to heaven. But he said as he departed, "I will come again the second time." We will all see him when he comes back to this earth again to claim his own.

WORDS: *Cherokee Hymn Book*; common phonetic transliteration by Marilyn M. Hofstra (Choctaw, Chickasaw) © 1992; Eng. paraphrase by Jennie Lee Fife (Cherokee) © 1992

Cheyenne Hymn

Jesus ne-ta wo-we ho-ni
Say-yo key-ya mi-yo-tigh
Say-yo kay-wo-wo-ni
She-hi tsoy-she
Aho ne-ta hay-tone.

WORDS: Trad. Cheyenne

Choctaw Hymn 48

Choctaw:

1. Shee-lom-bish Ho-lee-to-pah mah!
   Ish meen-tee pol-lah chah,
   Hah-tahk eel-buh-shah pee-ah h<u>ah</u>
   Ish pee yok-pah-lah-shkee.

2. Pee chok-osh no-see ah-tok-mah
   Ahnt ish ok-chuh-lah-shkee,
   Ish pee yo-bee-ee-cheek-bah-no;
   Ee cheem ah-uh-neh-shkee.

3 Shee-lom-bish Ho-lee-to-pah mah!
   Peem ah-nok-fee-lah huht
   Ok-theel-it kuh-nee-uh ho-kah,
   Ish-pee on to-mah-shkee.

4. Pee chok-ush nok-hahk-lo yo-kah
   Ahnt pee ho-po-luh-chee:
   Eel ah-uh-shuh-chee-kah yo-kah,
   Ish pee kah-sho-fah-shkee.

English paraphrase:

1. Come, O Holy Spirit!
   Come to us who are poor in spirit.
   Bless us!

2. Come and awaken our hearts.
   Give us your peace,
   we implore you.

3. O Holy Spirit!
   Our minds are clothed in darkness.
   Enlighten us!

4. Our hearts are filled with sorrow.
   Come and comfort us,
   sinners that we are.
   Cleanse us!

WORDS: Trad. Choctaw; common phonetic transliteration by Marilyn M. Hofstra (Choctaw, Chickasaw) © 1992; Eng. paraphrase by Harry Folsom (Choctaw) © 1992

Kiowa

Daw-k'ee dahay dawtsahy hee tsow'ah
Daw-k'ee dahay dawtsahy hee.
Bay dawtsahy-taw, gaw aym owthah t'aw.
Daw-k'ee dahay dawysahy h'ee.

WORDS: Trad. Kiowa

Mohawk Hymn

Mohawk: *English paraphrase:*

1. Jad kah thoh jee nee shon gwah
   wee.
   Nen yon gwee tee yo see.
   Ye yah gah wee ryah syah yo see.
   Skah nee gon rat ee genh.

2. Tee yon dah dee no ronh kwah see.
   KEE REES TOS shah go wee.
   Jee tyoh nah wah deht nee yo skahts.
   Wah don hehts hee ree yo.

3. Ka ya ne ren ka ronh ya geh.
   Ne sa ne ren honts ha.
   Ehn sa de tenh ston eh non ga.
   Ne jit kon di tye se.

4. Nee nee yo nah don ha hee ree.
   O nehn eh yee ya go.
   O nehn yah go noon dah ra on.
   Jee noon weh nee NEE YO.

1. See what he has given us
   to become a better person
   with a pure heart
   and of one mind.

2. Love one another.
   Christ has given
   his precious blood
   and his Holy Spirit

3. *(Could not be translated from
   Oneida to Mohawk to English)*

4. Now they are celebrating.
   She has arrived
   at the top of the mountain,
   at the place of Jesus.

WORDS: Mohawk translated from Oneida by Joe K. Peters; Eng. paraphrase by Emily White (Mohawk)
and Christi Garrow (Mohawk) © 1992

Muscogee Hymn 70

Muscogee (Creek):   *English paraphrase:*

1. Puyvfekcv Herat vhtet,
   Vnen vc vpvkvs;
   Cv feke ofvn vn likvs,
   Vm ohvtvliyvs.

2. Ekvnv vc vnokecat,
   Holwayeckv haken;
   Cv feket vn kawvpkvronks,
   Ce'cvkayecickvn.

3. Ehaperkvn ec oh huehkis,
   Cv feke kvsvppen,
   Vn yvhiketvt vn sumkeps,
   Cv tulas' onvpvn.

4. Yvn hesakiyet emunket
   Cv'stemerrusvr haks?
   Vm vnokeckvt yekcvronks;
   Cenaket yekcetvts.

1. Come, Holy Spirit, be with me.
   Dwell continually in my heart.

   *Stanzas 2, 3, and 4 have basically
   the same meaning as in the original English (see page 6).*

WORDS: *Muskokee Hymns*, Hymn 70; Eng. paraphrase by Leona Sullivan (Creek) © 1992

Navajo

1. Ni-zho-ni-go joo-ba' diits'a
   Yis-da-shiil-ti-ni-gii,
   Yoo-ii-yaa-nt-ee; k'ad she-nah- oos-dzin,
   Doo 'eesh'ii da nit'ee'.

2. Joo-ba' shi-jei sha nei-neez-taa'
   T'aa-bi sha ak'eh deesdlii'
   I-lii-go bi-joo-ba' yiil-tsa,
   T'oo yi-sis-dlaad yeedaa'.

3. T'oo-a-ha-yoi a-ti-'el-'i
   Bi-tah-dee' sheehoo-zin,
   Bi-joo-ba-'ii ei shi-laah neel'a,
   Ei bee baa nid-eesh-daal.

4. Neez-naa-di miil naa-hai ni-di
   Bi-ts'a-di'-ni-liid doo,
   Yool-kaa-lii ei doo bee bi-'oh da,
   Bee ha-hool-zhi-izh yee-doo.

WORDS: *Navajo Hymns of Faith*, phonetic transliteration by Albert Tsosie © 1992

Potawatomi

1. Nosk shehm-nit-to keem zhuh-wehn-mah,
   Gwis-sahn kee meen-go-nahn;
   Kee meek-wehn-mah ah-tee-mahk-see-yahn,
   Kos-nahn k'tah-ban-go-nahn.

2. Kshehm-nit-to gwis-sahn gee yah-wah,
   Shah-zhos keem zhin-kah-sot.
   Hehsh-pah-nah ween keem mnozh-jit-shkaht
   Ah-wee ko-wahb-mee-meht.

3. Meeg-wahtch-to-nahn ah-zhwan-mish-nok
   Ah-jah tah-mahk-see-yahk.
   Knob-maht-so-wehn mee-nah meesh-ko-swen
   K'tah-meen-goy-go jeh-yak.

WORDS: Transcription from trad. Potawatomi by James McKinney (Potawatomi) © 1992

Blest Be the Tie That Binds

1. Blest be the tie that binds our hearts in Chris - tian love; the fel - low - ship of kin - dred minds is like to that a - bove.
2. Be - fore our Fa - ther's throne we pour our ar - dent prayers; our fears, our hopes, our aims are one, our com - forts and our cares.
3. We share each oth - er's woes, our mut - ual bur - dens bear; and of - ten for each oth - er flows the sym - pa - thiz - ing tear.
4. When we a - sun - der part, it gives us in - ward pain; but we shall still be joined in heart, and hope to meet a - gain.

WORDS: John Fawcett
MUSIC: Johann G. Nägeli; arr. by Lowell Mason

Dakota Hymn 45

1. Wakantanka waste,
   Wacantkiya ece;
   Iyokisin yaun kinhan,
   Wacinyanpi waste.

2. Iye waonsida,
   Nakun wasaka ce;
   Cinca wicaye cin hena,
   Tanyan wicayuhe.

3. Cante sin unpi kin,
   Ito awacin po;
   Wakantanka nitawa kin
   Ehpeniyanpi sni.

WORDS: *Dakota Odowan: Dakota Hymns*

Inupiaq

Wales dialect (Alaska):

1. Quyanna miik killiiq simaaq tuat
   attausimun,
   Umatiivuut uqpishlum nagua gii tigai
   Maliguaq tii la ta atlausinagun
   tuuvuq sriliqgun,
   Pakmaaniiqtun illiglutaa.

2. Siugwani attataptaa agupiutain
   Uagut piisuuq taptiiqnun
   qanipsuuqtuut,
   Tallauqsralaavuut piumilaavuut
   piisuqtaavut attausiruu
   Asraaqtiut qaunaigut tigiin.

3. Illatni uagut avgua kaaluutaa
   Qaisilutaa illuptigun allianaamiik
   Aasiinuaguut attausinau shliugtut
   umatiivuut
   Paasrguutii qiiliiqsraap tiiqnun.

Phonetic transliteration:

1. Kwee-ah-na meek kee-leek see-
   mawk too-aht a-doe-see-moon,
   Oo-ma-tee-voot ook-pe-shloom nah-
   goo-ah gee tee gay
   Mah-lee-goo-awk tee lah dah ah-daw-
   see-nah goon too-vook she-leek-
   goon
   Bawk-mah-neek-toon-ee-lee-gloo-
   dah.

2. See-oo-gwah-nee adah-dap-dah ah-
   goo-pee-oo-tain
   Oo-ah-goot pee-zook dap-teek-noon
   kah-nip-soot-toot
   Tah-lok-shaw-lah-voot pee-oo-mee-
   law-voot pee-zook-tah-voot attow-
   see-rook
   Ah-shock-tee-oot ko-nay-goot tee-
   geen.

3. Ee-lawt-nee oo-ah-goot ahv-gwah
   caw-loo-dah
   Kay-see-loo-dah ee-loop-tee goon
   ah-lee-ah-nah-meek
   Ah-see-new-ah goot ah-do-see-no
   schlee-ook-toot oo-ma-tee-voot
   Pahsh-goo-tee keepleek-shawp teek-
   noon.

WORDS: Trad. Inupiaq; transcription and phonetic transliteration by John Pitney © 1992

Cesvs Purke Likan

♩ = 70

Refrain

Chee-sahs Polth-kee lay-kahn, Chee-sahs Polth-kee lay-kahn,

Chee-sahs Polth-kee lay-kahn, mahn tee-hee-chah-kah-thlees.

1. Mee-ko-sah - pahl - kee ah - pee - yah - nahn, Mee-ko-
2. Po - mah-pahl - tah - kee ah - pee - yah - nahn, Po - mah-
3. Elth-kee-nah - kahl - kee ah - pee - yah - nahn, Elth-kee-
4. Po - thlah-hahl - kee ah - pee - yah - nahn, Po -

sah - pahl - kee ah - pee - yah - nahn, Mee-ko-sah -
pahl - tah - kee ah - pee - yah - nahn, Po - mah-pahl -
nah - kahl - kee ah - pee - yah - nahn, Elth-kee-nah -
thlah - hahl - kee ah - pee - yah - nahn, Po - thlah -

pahl- kee ah-pee-yah - nahn, mahn tee - hee-chah - kah-thlees.
tah- kee ah-pee-yah - nahn, mahn tee - hee-chah - kah-thlees.
kahl- kee ah-pee-yah - nahn, mahn tee - hee-chah - kah-thlees.
hahl- kee ah-pee-yah - nahn, mahn tee - hee-chah - kah-thlees.

WORDS: Trad. Muscogee (Creek); common phonetic transliteration by Marilyn M. Hofstra (Choctaw, Chickasaw) © 1992; Eng. paraphrase by Leona Sullivan (Creek) © 1992

MUSIC: Trad. Muscogee (Creek); transcription by Marilyn M. Hofstra (Choctaw, Chickasaw) © 1992

Muscogee (Creek):

Refrain

Cesvs Purke likvn, Cesvs Purke likvn,
Cesvs Purke likvn mvn tehecvkvres.

1. Mekusvpvlke vpeyvnvn,
   Mekusvpvlke vpeyvnvn,
   Mekusvpvlke vpeyvnvn
   mvn tehecvkvres.
2. Pumvpvltvke ...
3. Erkenvkvlke ...
4. Purvkvlke ...
5. Pucusvlke ...
6. Puwvntvke ...
7. Hopuetvke ...

English paraphrase:

Refrain

Jesus our Father lives in heaven.
This is where we will see one
   another.

1. The laity have gone on ahead (to
   heaven); then we will see each other
   there.
2. Our friends ...
3. Ministers ...
4. Our elders ...
5. Our younger brothers/sisters ...
6. Our sisters ...
7. Our children ...

CRSHAW

Cherokee Hymn 26:
Guide Me, Jehovah

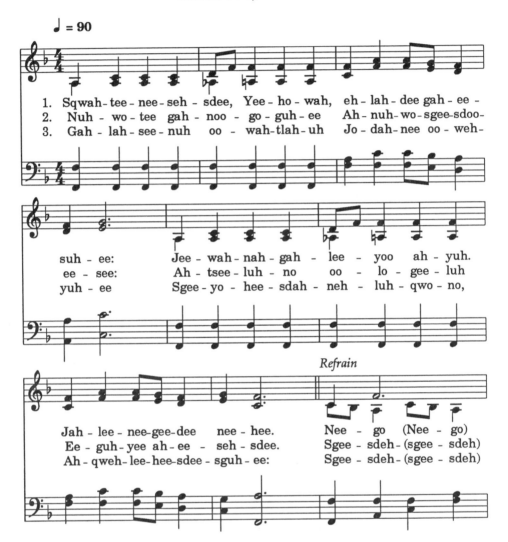

WORDS: William Williams; *Cherokee Hymn Book*; common phonetic transliteration by Marilyn M. Hofstra (Choctaw, Chickasaw) © 1992; Eng. paraphrase by Daniel Scott (Cherokee) © 1992

MUSIC: Trad. Cherokee; transcription and harm. by Marilyn M. Hofstra (Choctaw, Chickasaw) © 1992

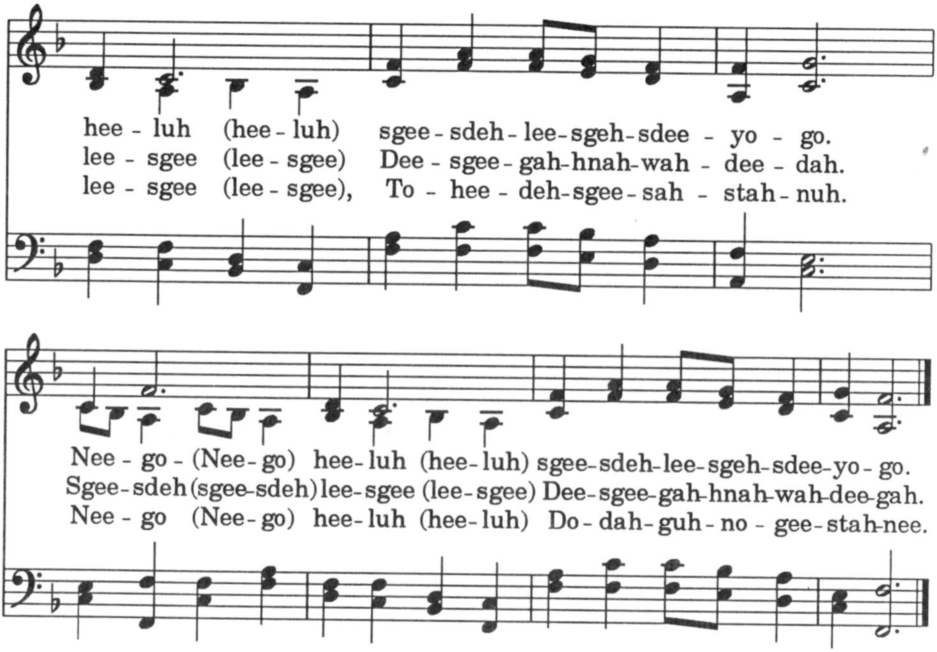
hee - luh (hee - luh) sgee - sdeh - lee - sgeh - sdee - yo - go.
lee - sgee (lee - sgee) Dee - sgee - gah-hnah-wah - dee - dah.
lee - sgee (lee - sgee), To - hee - deh-sgee - sah - stah - nuh.
Nee - go - (Nee - go) hee - luh (hee - luh) sgee-sdeh-lee-sgeh-sdee-yo - go.
Sgee-sdeh (sgee-sdeh) lee-sgee (lee - sgee) Dee-sgee-gah-hnah-wah-dee-gah.
Nee - go (Nee - go) hee - luh (hee - luh) Do - dah - guh - no - gee - stah-nee.

Cherokee:

1 ᏬᏆᎯᏂᏎᏬᏗ, ᏥᎰᏩ,
ᎡᏔᏗ ᎦᎢᏒᎢ:
ᏥᏨᏫᎦᏝᏳ ᎠᏰ.
ᏣᏝᏂᏱᏗ ᏂᎯ.
ᏂᎪᎯᏄ
ᏬᏱᏬᎦᏝᏬᎨᏬᏗᏲᎪ.

2 ᎤᏇᏘ ᎦᏄᎪᎡᎢ
ᎠᎤᏇ ᏳᏱᏬᏍᎢᏏ:
ᎠᏥᏄᏃ ᎤᏣᏱᏄ
ᎢᎬᏍ ᎠᎢᏎᏬᏗ.
ᏬᏱᏬᎦᏝᏬᏱ
ᏗᏬᏱᎦᏥᏩᏗᏏ.

3 ᎹᏔᏏᎤ ᎤᏩᏞᎢ
ᏦᏓᏂ ᎤᏪᏰᎢ
ᏬᏱᏲᎯᏬᏓᏁᏄᏑᏃ,
ᎠᏇᏝᎯᏳᏗᏬᎨᎢ:
ᏬᏱᏬᎦᏝᏳᏱ,
ᏙᎯ ᎦᏳᏱᏌᏳᏔᎤ.
ᏂᎪᎯᏄ
ᏙᏓᎡᏃᏱᏬᏔᏂ.

English paraphrase:

1. Take me and guide me, Jehovah, as I am walking through this barren land. I am weak, but thou art mighty. Ever help us.
2. Open unto us thy healing waters. Let the fiery cloud (Holy Spirit) go before us and continue thy help.
3. Help us when we come to the Jordan River (death) and we shall sing thy praise eternally.

Cherokee Hymn 36: Heaven Beautiful

WORDS: *Cherokee Hymn Book*; common phonetic transliteration by Marilyn M. Hofstra (Choctaw, Chickasaw) © 1992; Eng. paraphrase, stanzas by Daniel Scott (Cherokee) © 1973, refrain by Jennie Lee Fife (Cherokee) © 1992

MUSIC: Trad. Cherokee; transcription and harm. by Marilyn M. Hofstra (Choctaw, Chickasaw) © 1992

Cherokee:

1 ᎤᏁᎳᏅᎯ ᎤᏪᏥ
ᏂᎦᏗ ᎡᏗᎨᏳᎢ
ᎿᏉ ᏗᏓᎸᏭ,
ᏧᎶᏒ ᎢᏓᎢᏎᏍᏗ,
ᏕᎦᏓᏂᏴᏎᏍᏗᏃ,
ᏗᎦᏓᎨᏳᎯ.

2 ᎤᎬᏫᏳᎯ ᎤᏤᎵ
ᏕᏗᎧᎿᏩᏗᏎᏍᏗ
ᎠᏂ ᎡᎶ.Ꭿ ᎨᏒ;
ᏌᏉᏃ ᎸᏍᏗᏗᏎᏍᏗ;
ᏥᏌ ᎦᎶᏁᏛ ᎾᏍᎩ
ᏕᎦᏘᏂᏎᏍᏗ.

3 ᎣᏒ ᎢᎩᏙᎵᏨᎯ
ᎡᏓᎵᎡᎵᏤᎵᏍᏗ
ᏂᎪᎯᎸ ᎿᏉ;
ᏩᏙᎯᏳ ᎣᎩᏰᎸ
ᎠᏎ ᎢᎩᏍᏕᎸᏗᏉ,
ᎤᏁᏨᎯᏰᏃ.

4 ᎤᏁᎳᏅᎯ ᎤᏪᏥ
ᏧᏪᏙᎵᏍᏗᏉ ᎠᏎ
ᎬᏩᏔᏲᏎᎯ;
ᎢᎦᏛᎦᏅᎯᏰᏃ
ᎸᏍᏛᏉ ᎢᏕᏭ ᎠᏂ,
ᎤᏲᏍᏛᏉᏰᏃ.

5 ᏰᏗᏔᏏᏘᏬ ᏥᏌ,
ᏬᏲ ᎢᎦᎵᏍᏓᏁᏗ
ᎿᏆᏎ, ᎤᏁᏨ,
ᎸᏃᎯᏳᏅᎾ ᎣᎩ
ᏓᏳᎾᎸᎾᏓ ᎠᏎ,
ᎤᏛᏅᎯ ᏥᏌ

6 ᎤᏁᎳᏅᎯ ᎤᏪᏥ
ᎯᎠ ᏂᎩᏪᏎᎸᎢ;
ᎠᏴ ᏍᎩᏍᏓᏩᏚᎦ,
ᏓᏥᏩᏛᎯᏉ ᎠᏎ
ᏫᎾᏍᏛᎾ ᎢᎦᎦᏘ
ᎦᎸᎳᏗ ᏦᏒ.Ꭲ.

English paraphrase:

1. Let us who love the Son of God rise up and follow him in love.
2. Let us look to the ways of the Lord while we are still on this earth, and the Lord Jesus Christ shall lead us.
3. Let us continually give thanks unto him who had mercy upon us.
4. The Son of God came into the world. The world was evil: the world knew him not. He called and we heard him.

Refrain

Heaven beautiful they are saying. Jehovah they are yours; there is no sin and it does not exist in heaven.

Cherokee Hymn 87: Christ's Second Coming

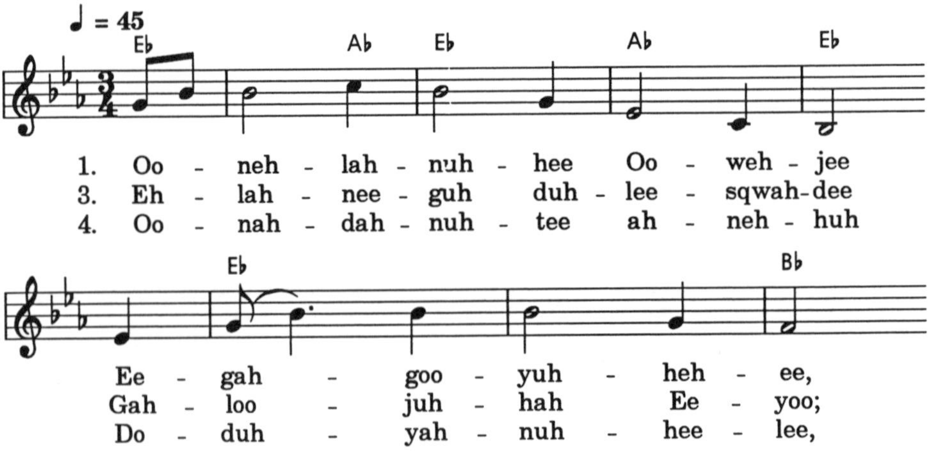

Words can also be sung to "Amazing Grace" and "It Came Upon a Midnight Clear"

WORDS: *Cherokee Hymn Book;* common phonetic transliteration by Marilyn M. Hofstra (Choctaw, Chickasaw) © 1992; Eng. paraphrase by Jennie Lee Fife (Cherokee) © 1992

MUSIC: Trad. Cherokee; transcription by Marilyn M. Hofstra (Choctaw, Chickasaw) © 1992

hnah - qwo jo - suh wee - oo - lo - seh
Nee - gah - dee dah - yeh - dee - go - ee
Jo - eh hnah - qwo nee - go - hee - luh

Ee - gah goo - yuh - ho - nuh. *(to 2)*
Ah - nee eh - lah - nee - guh. *(to 4)*
Do - hee wah - neh - heh - sdee.

2. Ee - seh - no ee - oo - neh - jeh - ee

Ah - yoo - no doo - leh - nuh,

Tah - lee - neh duh - jee - loo - jee - lee,

Oo - duh - - neh - oo - neh - juh. *(to 3)*

Cherokee:

1 ᎤᎳᏬᎥᎠ ᎤᏍᎩ
ᏔᏗᎦᏓᎢᏘ,
ᏂᏳ ᏦᎡ ᎣᎤᎦᏘ
ᏔᏗᏴᎭᎥ.

2 ᏔᏲᏃ ᎢᎤᎳᏨᏘ
ᎠᏓᏃ ᏴᏙ,
ᏪᎵᎠ ᎦᎿᎷᎵᎡ.
ᎤᎿᎵᎠ ᎤᎵᏞ.

3 ᏣᎥᎮᎬ ᎦᎵᎿᏔᏗ
ᏍᎻᏣᎢ ᏔᏆ;
ᎮᏍᎵ ᎤᏱᏗᎠᎢ
ᎠᎭ ᏣᎥᎮᎬ.

4 ᎤᎦᏙᏗᎠ ᎠᎳᏍ
ᎥᎳᏍᏲᎠᎵ,
ᎦᎡ ᏂᏳ ᎲᎵᎵᏆ
ᎥᎠ ᏣᎵᎶᏍᏘ.

English paraphrase:

Jesus, Son of God, paid the price for us and now he has gone on to heaven. But he said as he departed, "I will come again the second time." We will all see him when he comes back to this earth again to claim his own.

Chippewa Hymn 26:
Come, Thou Fount of Every Blessing

♩ = 80

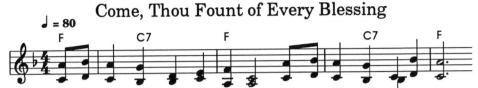

1. Oon dah shon suh, ta bain duh mun, Ke che zhuh wain je ga win;
2. Kee gee duh gwe shim suh o mah Che zhee be ne ka too non;
3. Oh ka gait zhuh wain je ga win, Ning e che muh ze nuh aun!

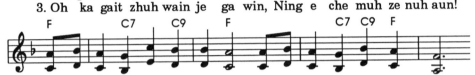

Wuh wa zhe toon mon duh nin da, Che nuh nuh guh mo too non
E na ne *me* wuh nan dush go Mee nuh wah ning uh kee way;
Mon oo zah ge e de win ing, Min je muh pe doon nin da:

Ke ke noo uh muh we shin suh, Ish pe ming na g-uh mo wod;
Je sus ning ee me kog ma gwah Puh bah wah ne s-he nom bon;
Na tah wuh ne she noong in suh Nin de zhe ke d-e mah gis:

Ke che me gwaich min je mee yon Ke zhuh wain je ga win ing!
Mee ewh nun nee zah ne ze yon Kah oon je ne bo tuh wid!
Ke mee nin nin da, Oh mon oo, O dah pe nuh muh we shin.

Original English:

1. Come, thou Fount of every blessing,
tune my heart to sing thy grace;
streams of mercy, never ceasing,
call for songs of loudest praise.
Teach me some melodious sonnet,
sung by flaming tongues above.
Praise the mount! I'm fixed upon it,
mount of thy redeeming love.

2. Here I raise mine Ebenezer;
hither by thy help I'm come;
and I hope, by thy good pleasure,
safely to arrive at home.
Jesus sought me when a stranger,
wandering from the fold of God;
he, to rescue me from danger,
interposed his precious blood.

3. O to grace, how great a debtor
daily I'm constrained to be!
Let thy goodness, like a fetter,
bind my wandering heart to thee.
Prone to wander, Lord, I feel it,
prone to leave the God I love;
here's my heart, O take and seal it,
seal it for thy courts above.

WORDS: Robert Robinson; *Chippeway and English Hymns*
MUSIC: Trad. Chippewa; transcription and harm. by Glenna Willis © 1992

Chippewa Hymn 47:
A Charge to Keep I Have

♩ = 75

1. Che   uh no kee too   non,   Noo sa nin duh yah   nun;
2. Wuh   wa zhe e shin   suh   Che uh gah san' mo   yon;

Che wee kee zhee tod nin je   chog   Ish   pe ming wee e   zhod.
Che   da kee zhee tah yon, Noo   sa,   Uh   pee nuh qua shkoo non.

Ke nun duh wa   nim   suh   Che uh   no   kee too non,
Wee doo kuh we   shin   suh,   Che uh   kuh wah be yon,

Oh mon oo ong wah me   e   shin, Qui yuk che 'num' ah   yon.
Kuh ya che uh nuh me   ah yon, Wee pe mah de   ze   yon.

Original English:

1. A charge to keep I have,
   a God to glorify,
   a never-dying soul to save,
   and fit it for the sky.
   To serve the present age,
   my calling to fulfill;
   O may it all my powers engage
   to do my Master's will!

2. Arm me with jealous care,
   as in thy sight to live,
   and oh, thy servant, Lord, prepare
   a strict account to give!
   Help me to watch and pray,
   and on thyself rely,
   assured, if I my trust betray,
   I shall forever die.

WORDS: Charles Wesley; *Chippeway and English Hymns*; common phonetic transliteration by William A. Cargo and Frances Rhodes © 1992

MUSIC: Trad. Chippewa (Ojibway); harm. by Frances Rhodes; transcription by William A. Cargo © 1992

Choctaw Hymn 21:
Sinners, Can You Hate the Savior?

(Tune: Press Along)

1. Uh - buh peen Chee - to - kah - kah yuht,
2. Yo - sho - bah bee - ee - kah ho - chah
3. Kuh - nah kee - ah pee nok - hahk - lo

O eel - ee ko - steen - een - chee,"
Ah - yok - pol - lo - kah fee - nah
Pee ok - chah - leen - chah hee - uht

Eet peem ah - hahn - chee - pol - lah kah
Ee chah - ko - wah ho - see ho - nah,
Eek - sho; Chee - suhs ahk bah - no tok;

Ee - ho hahk - lo pol - lah - shkee.
Pee nok hahk - lo tok o - kee.
Ee - ho ho - lee - tob - lah - shkee.

WORDS: *Choctaw Hymn Book*; common phonetic transliteration by Marilyn M. Hofstra (Choctaw, Chicka-saw) © 1992; Eng. paraphrase by Harry D. Folsom (Choctaw) © 1992

MUSIC: Trad. Choctaw; transcription by Marilyn M. Hofstra (Choctaw, Chickasaw) © 1992

Choctaw:

1. Uba pin Chitokaka, yut,
   "Oh ile kostininchi,"
   Et pim ahanchi pulla ka
   Eho haklo pullashke.

Refrain:

   Hatak yoshoba pia hut
   Pin Chisus achukma ka
   Il i nukilla hinla cho?
   Anukfillit ke pisa.

2. Yoshoba bieka hocha
   Aiokpuloka fehna
   E chukowa hosi hona,
   Pi nukhaklo tok oke.

3. Kuna kia pi nukhaklot
   Pi okchalincha hi ut
   Iksho; Chisus ak bano tok:
   Eho holitoblashke.

English paraphrase:

1. The Lord up above says to us, "Let us be of one spiritual mind." He is merciful. Therefore, let us hear his word.

Refrain:

   Sinners, our Jesus is so good and kind, how can you hate him? Let us meditate on these things.

2. Even though we are lost and headed for destruction, still he has mercy upon us.

3. There is no other who has mercy and can save us—only Jesus. Let us praise him.

Choctaw Hymn 21:
Sinners, Can You Hate the Savior?

♩ = 75

1. Uh - buh peen Chee - to - kah - kah, yuht, "O eel
2. Yo - sho - bah bee - ee - kah ho - chah Ah - yok
3. Kuh - nah kee - ah pee nok - hahk - lo Pee ok

ee ko - steen-een - chee," Eet - peem ah - hahn-chee pol -
poh - lo - kah fee - nah Ee chah-ko - wah ho - see
chah-leen-chah hee uht Eek-sho; Chee-suhs ahk bah-

lah kah Ee - ho hahk - lo pol - lah - shkee.
ho - nah, Pee nok - hahk - lo tok o - kee.
no tok: Ee - ho ho - lee - tob - lah - shkee.

Refrain

Hah-tahk yo-sho (Hah-tahk yo - sho) bah pee-ah hut (pee-ah

huht) Peen Chee-suhs (Peen Chee-ee-suhs) ah-chok-mah kah (ah-chok-mah

kah) Eel-ee nok-kee (Eel-ee nok-kee) lah heen-lah cho? (heen-lah

cho) Ah - nok - feel - leet kee pee - sah.

See page 23 for English paraphrase

WORDS: *Choctaw Hymn Book*; common phonetic transliteration by Marilyn M. Hofstra (Choctaw, Chicka-saw) © 1992; Eng. paraphrase by Harry D. Folsom (Choctaw) © 1992

MUSIC: Trad. Choctaw; transcription and harm. by Marilyn M. Hofstra (Choctaw, Chickasaw) © 1992

Choctaw Hymn 35

1. Chee - suhs pol - lah kuh - to
2. Yahk - nee lo - sah ho - kah
3. Yo - mo - mee po - lah muht,

Pee nok - hahk - lo ho - chah,
Ahnt ah - hahn - tah ho - kuht,
Chee - suhs pol - lah hah - sh osh,

Een - kee Chee - ho - wah ees - sah chah,
Ok - lah eel - buh - shah pee - sah muht,
"Uhth-toh - buht suhl - lee pol - lah - shkee."

Meen - tee uh - lah hah - tok.
Nok - hahk - lo tok o - kee.
Ah - hahn - chee tok o - kee.

Choctaw:

1. Chisus pulla kuto
   Pi nukhaklo hocha,
   Iki Chihowa issa cha,
   Mintit ula hatok.

2. Yakni lusa hoka
   Ant ahanta hokut,
   Okla ilbusha pisa mut,
   Nukhaklo tok oke.

3. Yumohmi pula mut,
   Chisus pulla hash osh,
   "Ulhtobut sulli pullashke."
   Ahanchi tok oke.

English paraphrase:

1. Jesus is merciful. Even though we may have turned away from God, he came for that reason.

2. He came and dwelt among us on this earth, and because he saw the people suffering he had mercy upon them.

3. When the time came for his purpose to be fulfilled, he said, "By my death I have paid the price for you." This is what he says to us.

WORDS: *Choctaw Hymn Book*; common phonetic transliteration by Marilyn M. Hofstra (Choctaw, Chickasaw) © 1992; Eng. paraphrase by Harry D. Folsom (Choctaw) © 1992
MUSIC: Trad. Choctaw; transcription by Marilyn M. Hofstra (Choctaw, Chickasaw) © 1992

Choctaw Hymn 112: Meditation on Death

♩ = 50

1. Nee - tahk kah - nee - mah - fee - nah ho
2. Chee - suhs pol - lah tok mahk o - nah,
3. Chee - ho - wah pol - lah kahk o - chah

See - ah - eel - lee hok - mah,
See - ah - eel - lee hok - muht,
Ah nok - hahk - lo hok - mah,

Ah - kee uh - buh bee - nee - lee muht
Uh - buh yahk - nee ah - chok - mah kah
Uh - buh yahk - nee peel - lah ho - kah

Ees sah hah - lahn - lah - shkee.
O - nah lah hee o - kee.
O - nah lah hee o - kee.

Choctaw:

1. Nitak kanima fehna ho
   Si ai illi hokma,
   Aki uba binili mut
   Is sa halanlashke.

2. Chisus pulla tuk mak ona,
   Si ai illi hokmut,
   uba yakni achukma ka
   Ona la hi oke.

3. Chihowa pulla kak ocha
   Anukhaklo hokma,
   Uba yakni pilla hoka
   One la hi oke.

English paraphrase:

1. When it comes my appointed day to die, the Father up above will take me by the hand and receive me.

2. Jesus our Lord abides in that good land above (heaven). I will go there.

3. Our merciful God abides in heaven above. I will go there.

WORDS: *Choctaw Hymn Book*; common phonetic transliteration by Marilyn M. Hofstra (Choctaw, Chickasaw) © 1992; Eng. paraphrase by Harry D. Folsom (Choctaw) © 1992
MUSIC: Trad. Choctaw; transcription by Marilyn M. Hofstra (Choctaw, Chickasaw) © 1992

Choctaw Hymn 138: The Gospel

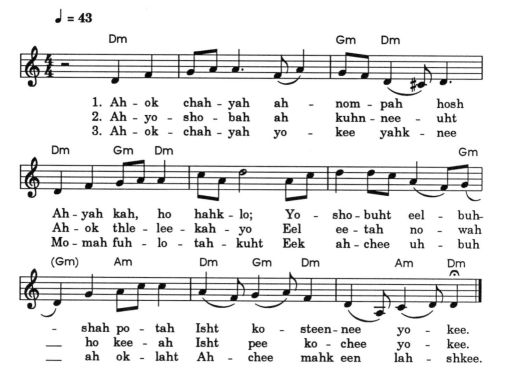

Choctaw:

1. Aiok chaya anumpa hosh
   Aya ka, ho haklo;
   Yoshobut ilbusha puta
   Isht kostini yoke.

2. Ayoshoba a kuniut
   Aiokhlilika yo
   Il itunowa hoh kia
   Isht pi kuchi yoke.

3. Aiokcyaya yoke yakni
   Moma fullota kut
   Ik achi; uba ai okla't
   Achi mak inlashke.

English paraphrase:

1. Hear the message of the Living
   Word, you who are lost and suffering
   will be changed.

2. Though we are lost and wander in
   darkness, he will bring us forth out of
   darkness.

3. To all the world, what is done will
   be as in heaven. It is said, it will be so.

WORDS: *Choctaw Hymn Book;* common phonetic transliteration by Marilyn M. Hofstra (Choctaw, Chickasaw) © 1992; Eng. paraphrase by Jacob S. Bohanon (Choctaw) HIJC, Lawrence, KS © 1992
MUSIC: Trad. Choctaw; transcription by Marilyn M. Hofstra (Choctaw, Chickasaw) © 1992

Come and Go with Me to That Land

Caddo:

1. Ke-wht ha-U nah-tse de-sah
   Nah Ah-ah nah Ah-ah,
   Ke-wht ha-U nah-tse de-sah
   Nah Ah-ah.

2. Hay sah-yah ko-tse de-sah ...

3. Ha-ah-hutt khn-hay-ay ...

4. Ha-ah-hutt khn-oos sin-nah ...

English paraphrase:

1. My home in heaven is where I'm going, come and go where I'm bound with the Father.

2. It's a good place there with the Father, come and go ...

3. You feel good and loving with the Father, ...

4. All you people should come and listen to the Father, ...

WORDS: Caddo text by Kenneth Edmonds (Caddo) © 1992; Eng. translation by Prudy Pewenofkit (Caddo) © 1992; common phonetic transliteration by Marilyn M. Hofstra (Choctaw, Chickasaw) © 1991

MUSIC: Adpt. from African-American gospel song; transcription by Marilyn M. Hofstra (Choctaw, Chickasaw) © 1992

Dakota Hymn 141: Many and Great, O God

1. Man-y and great, O God, are thy things, Mak-er of earth and sky. Thy hands have set the heav-ens with stars; thy fin-gers spread the moun-tains and plains. Lo, at thy word the wa-ters were formed; deep seas o-bey thy voice.

2. Grant un-to us com-mun-ion with thee, thou star a-bid-ing one; come un-to us and dwell with us; with thee are found the gifts of life. Bless us with life that has no end, e-ter-nal life with thee.

Suggested percussion part for hand drum:

Dakota:

1. Wakantanka taku nitawa
   Tankaya qa ota;
   Mahpiya kin eyahnake ca,
   Maka kin he duowanca,
   Mniowanca sbeya wanke cin,
   Hena oyakihi.

2. Nitawacin wasaka, wakan,
   On wawicahyaye;
   Woyute qa wokoyake kin,
   Woyatke ko iyacinyan,
   Anpetu kin otoiyohi
   Wawiyohiyaye.

WORDS: *Dakota Odowan: Dakota Hymns*, Hymn 141 by Joseph R. Renville; paraphrase by Philip Frazier
MUSIC: Trad. Dakota

Euchee Hymn

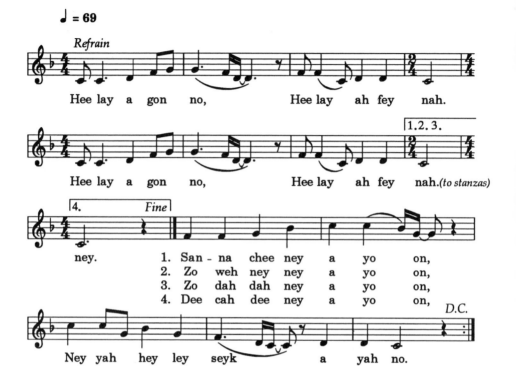

♩ = 69

Refrain

Hee lay a gon no,   Hee lay ah fey nah.

Hee lay a gon no,   Hee lay ah fey nah. *(to stanzas)*

1.2.3.

4. **Fine**

ney.

1. San - na chee ney a yo on,
2. Zo weh ney ney a yo on,
3. Zo dah dah ney a yo on,
4. Dee cah dee ney a yo on,

D.C.

Ney yah hey ley seyk a yah no.

Euchee:

Refrain

He lay a gono, He lay ah fey nah.
He lay a gono, He lay ah fey nah.

1. Sanna che ney a yon
   Ney yah hey ley seyk a yah no.

2. Zo weh ney ney a yon, ...

3. Zo dah dah ney a yon ...

4. De cah de ney a yon ...

English translation:

Refrain

Let everyone come, let everyone go.
Let everyone come, let everyone go.

1. Christians, do not fall or turn back.

2. Sisters, do not fall or turn back.

3. Brothers, ...

4. My friends, ...

WORDS: Trad. Euchee; common phonetic transliteration by Marilyn M. Hofstra (Choctaw, Chickasaw)
© 1992; Eng. translation by Maxine Barnett (Euchee) © 1992
MUSIC: Trad. Euchee; transcription by Marilyn M. Hofstra (Choctaw, Chickasaw) © 1992

Face to Face

1. Face to face with Christ, my Savior, face to face—what
2. Only faintly now, I see him, with the darkling
3. What rejoicing in his presence, when are banished
4. Face to face! O blissful moment! Face to face— to

will it be? When with rapture I behold him, Jesus
veil between, but a blessed day is coming, when his
grief and pain; when the crooked ways are straightened, and the
see and know; face to face with my Redeemer, Jesus

Refrain

Christ who died for me.
glory shall be seen.
dark things shall be plain. Face to face I shall behold him,
Christ who loves me so.

far beyond the starry sky; face to face in all his

glory, I shall see him by and by!

WORDS: Mrs. Frank A. Breck
MUSIC: Grant Colfax Tullar

Mohawk

<table>
<tr><td>Mohawk:</td><td>English translation:</td></tr>
<tr><td>

1. Te hi ka ne re ne YE SOS.
   Tsi ro ia ta ne ra kwat.
   Te hi ka ne re ne YE SOS.
   Ne ne ra kwen he ia se.

Refrain

   Enhi kenon te ken ni ih.
   No nen e to ien ke we.
   En hi kenon te ken ni ih.
   Ne ne shon kwen he ia se.

2. Nek ne ia kenne tsi ri kens.
   Tsi io ta sa ta ra kes.
   Ta we tsi wen ni se ra te.
   Ien ke we tsi ten te ron.

3. O nen wa ka ton ha he re.
   Ne YE SOS ra ia tak tha.
   A kwe kon e ren wa kawi ton.
   Ka ni kon rak sen se ra.

4. Ia ke ni kwe kon ne YE SOS.
   Ne ne ra ke no ron kwa.
   O nen ne ies ha kia ta kwen.
   KE RIS TOS shak ne ren shon.

</td><td>

1. I am looking at Jesus.
   He is so wonderful.
   I am looking at Jesus.
   He gave his life for me.

Refrain

   Will I see him
   when I get there?
   Will I see him,
   he who died for us?

2. I barely see him
   in the passing shadow.
   The day will come
   when I arrive at his place.

3. Now I am celebrating
   by the side of Jesus.
   I have removed all
   my unpleasant thoughts.

4. We are together, Jesus.
   He who loves me,
   he has redeemed me.
   Christ has freed me.

</td></tr>
</table>

WORDS: Transcription from trad. Mohawk by Joe K. Peters (verse 3, line 3 revised by White and Garrow); Eng. translation by Emily White (Mohawk) and Christie Garrow (Mohawk) © 1992

He Loves Me

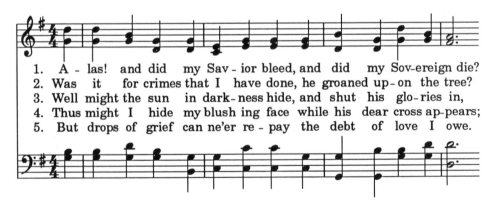

1. A - las! and did my Sav - ior bleed, and did my Sov-ereign die?
2. Was it for crimes that I have done, he groaned up-on the tree?
3. Well might the sun in dark-ness hide, and shut his glo-ries in,
4. Thus might I hide my blush ing face while his dear cross ap-pears;
5. But drops of grief can ne'er re - pay the debt of love I owe.

WORDS: Isaac Watts; refrain anon.
MUSIC: Anon.

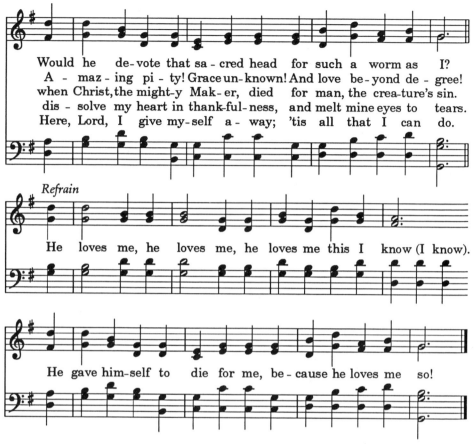

Would he de-vote that sa-cred head for such a worm as I?
A - maz - ing pi - ty! Grace un-known! And love be-yond de - gree!
when Christ, the might-y Mak- er, died for man, the crea-ture's sin.
dis - solve my heart in thank-ful-ness, and melt mine eyes to tears.
Here, Lord, I give my-self a - way; 'tis all that I can do.

Refrain

He loves me, he loves me, he loves me this I know (I know).

He gave him-self to die for me, be - cause he loves me so!

Choctaw Hymn 120: Judgment

Choctaw:

1. Ne-tahk ish-tah-e-yo-pik-muh-no,
   Che-suhs uht me-hen-teh,
   "Uhm uhl-ah ho-le-to-pah mah!
   Che hoht ah-yah lish-ke."

*Refrain**

   Ah hohl-lo, ah-hohl-lo,
   Ah-hohl-lo fee-nah-shkee.
   Si ulth-to-buht pee-ah-huht
   Ah hohl-lo fee-nah-shkee.

2. "Chem ah-yah-shah ik-be le hosh
   E-yah le tok-o-chah,
   Chem ah-tah-yah-le le tok-osh,
   Che hoht uhl-ah lish-ke."

3. Che-suhs uht ah-chah he o-ke;
   Ill-uhp-pah hahk-lo-muht
   Che-suhs e yem-me ah-le kuht
   Nah yok-pah he o-ke.

English paraphrase:

1. On the day of judgment, Jesus will
   come saying these words, "My
   precious children, I have come to take
   you."

Refrain

   He loves me, he loves me,
   he loves me, this I know.
   He gave himself to die for me,
   because he loves me so!

2. "For you, each of you, I have
   prepared a place. It is for this purpose
   I left you before. Now it is ready, I
   have come to take you."

3. These are the words of Jesus; now
   all must hear. If you hear and believe
   in Jesus there shall be great joy.

* *The English words to the refrain may be sung instead of the Choctaw*

WORDS: *Choctaw Hymn Book*; Eng. paraphrase by Jacob Bohanon (Choctaw) © 1992

Heleluyan: Hallelujah

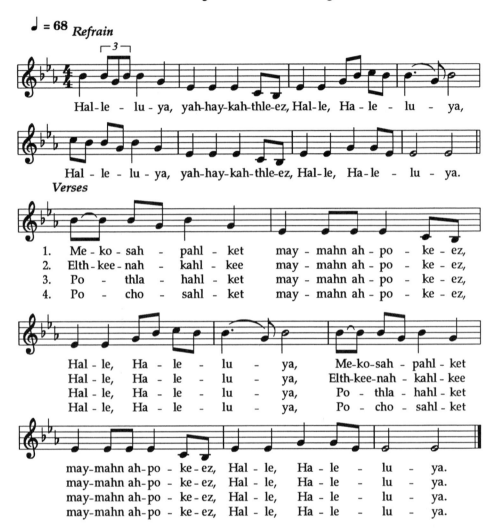

WORDS: Trad. Muscogee (Creek); common phonetic transliteration by Marilyn M. Hofstra (Choctaw, Chickasaw) © 1992; Eng. paraphrase by Leona Sullivan (Creek) © 1992

MUSIC: Trad. Muscogee (Creek); transcription by Marilyn M. Hofstra (Choctaw, Chickasaw) © 1992

Muscogee (Creek):

Refrain

Heleluyvn yvhikvres, hele heleluyvn,
Heleluyvn yvhikvres, hele heleluyvn.

1. Mekosapvlket mimvn vpokes,
   hele heleluyvn,
   Mekosapvlket mimvn vpokes,
   hele heleluyvn.
2. Erkenakvlke ...
3. Purahvlket ...
4. Pucusvlket ...
5. Puwantaket (Po-wahn-tah-ket) ...
6. Hopuetaket (Ho-po-e-tah-ket) ...
7. Vkvsamvlket (Uh-kuh-sah-mul-ket) ...
8. Emestvlket (E-mes-tuhl-ket) ...
9. Pumetvlwvlket (Po-me-tuhl-wuhl-ket) ...

English paraphrase:

Refrain

I will sing hallelujah,
I will sing hallelujah.

1. Christian people are there (in
   heaven) and I will sing hallelujah
   with them when I get there.

2. The ministers ...
3. The elders ...
4. The younger ones ...
5. Our sisters ...
6. Our children ...
7. Believers ...

8. God's people ...
9. Our communities ...

CRSHAW

Hvlwen Heckvyofvn

♩ = 78

Refrain

Hahl - wehn   Heech - kah-ee-yo - fahn,   hahl - wehn

Heech - kah-ee-yo - fahn,   Hahl - wehn   Heech   *Fine*

kah-ee-yo - fahn,   Hee - sah - kee-tah - mee - see.

1. Mee-ko-sah - pahl - keht   mee-ko-sah - pah   Mee-ko -
2. Elth-kee-nah - kahl - kee   mee-ko-sah - pah   Elth-kee -
3. Po - thlah - hahl - keht   mee-ko-sah - pah   Po -
4. Po - cho - sahl - keht   mee-ko-sah - pah   Po -
5. Ho - po-ee - tah - keht   mee-ko-sah - pah   Ho -

sah - pahl - keht   ahyee - mah - hah   Hahl -
nah - kahl - kee   ahyee - mah - hah   Hahl -
thlah - hahl - keht   ahyee - mah - hah   Hahl -
cho - sahl - keht   ahyee - mah - hah   Hahl -
po - ee - tah - keht   ahyee - mah - hah   Hahl -

D.C.

wee   tah - lo - fah   mi - mahn.   Hahl - wehn
wee   tah - lo - fah   mi - mahn.   Hahl - wehn
wee   tah - lo - fah   mi - mahn.   Hahl - wehn
wee   tah - lo - fah   mi - mahn.   Hahl - wehn
wee   tah - lo - fah   mi - mahn.   Hahl - wehn

WORDS: Trad. Muscogee (Creek); common phonetic transliteration by Marilyn M. Hofstra (Choctaw, Chickasaw) © 1992; Eng. paraphrase by Leona Sullivan (Creek) © 1992

MUSIC: Trad. Muscogee (Creek); transcription by Marilyn M. Hofstra (Choctaw, Chickasaw) © 1992

Muscogee (Creek):

Refrain

Hvlwen Heckvyofvn,
Hvlwen Heckvyofvn,
Hvlwen Heckvyofvn,
Hesaketvmese.

1. Mekusapvlke mekusapv
   Mekusapvlke ayemvhvs
   Hvlwe tvlofv minvn.

2. Erkenvkvlke ...

3. Purahvlke ...

4. Pucusvlke ...

5. Hopuetake ...

English Paraphrase:

Refrain

Giver of Breath, born on high.

1. Christian people keep on praying
   and pressing on to heaven.

2. Ministers ...

3. Older brothers and sisters ...

4. Younger brothers and sisters ...

5. Children ...

Our family is very large.

It extends beyond the ties of blood.
It reaches out to the old, the young,
the stranger, the orphan.

(There's room for all.)

Jesus, Lover of My Soul

1. Je - sus, lov - er of my soul, let me to thy bos-om fly,
2. Oth - er ref - uge have I none, hangs my help-less soul on thee;
3. Thou, O Christ, art all I want, more than all in thee I find;
4. Plen-teous grace with thee is found, grace to cov - er all my sin;

while the near-er wat - ers roll, while the temp-est still is high.
leave, ah! leave me not a - lone, still sup-port and com-fort me.
raise the fall-en, cheer the faint, heal the sick, and lead the blind.
let the heal-ing streams a-bound, make and keep me pure with - in.

Hide me, O my Sav-ior, hide, till the storm of life is past;
All my trust on thee is stayed, all my help from thee I bring;
Just and ho - ly is thy name, I am all un-righ-teous-ness;
Thou of life the foun-tain art, free-ly let me take of thee;

safe in - to the ha - ven guide; O re-ceive my soul at last.
cov - er my de-fense-less head with the shad-ow of thy wing.
false and full of sin I am; thou art full of truth and grace.
spring thou up with-in my heart; rise to all e - ter - ni - ty.

WORDS: Charles Wesley
MUSIC: Simeon B. Marsh

Choctaw Hymn 55: Christians Hope

Choctaw:

1. Uh-bah Me-ko- pul-lah kah
   Im uhl-lah huh-che-ah mah!
   Tah-lo-ah ho-le-to-pah
   Huhsh tah-lo-ah pul-lah-shke:

2. Huhsh tah-lo-ho-wah ho-kuht
   Che-suhs huh-che ho-huh-lo,
   Huh-che ok-chah-lin-che kah,
   Huhsh im ah-nah-yah-chah-shke.

3. Huh-chish-no fe-nah luh-to
   Uh-bah a-ho-le-to-pah.
   Huhsh i ah-nah-tah he uht
   Uh-bah tah-lah-yah ho-ke.

4. Che-suhs ah e-ah-kah-e-yuht
   Uh-bah yah huhsh o-nah chah,
   Nahn isht ill-i-yok-pah mah
   Huhsh pe-sah mahk in-lah-shke.

English Paraphrase:

1. Our King of above
   whose children you are!
   You must all sing
   this holy song.

2. Thou shall ask in
   your song that
   "Jesus so love you,
   He shall save you."

3. For each of you
   the heavenly place
   where ye shall dwell
   is there for you.

4. Follow Jesus to
   the heavenly place.
   You will see joy such
   as you have never seen.

WORDS: *Choctaw Hymn Book;* Eng. paraphrase by Jacob Bohanon (Choctaw) © 1992

Dakota Hymn 79

1. Jesus onsimada kin,
   Niye en onawapa;
   Taku sica ota hin,
   Hena en maun esta,
   Jesus niye on wani,
   Niye hinwacinciye;
   Hecen nis tohan yahi,
   Miye onsimada ye.

2. Wowinape tokeca
   Takudan yuhapi sni;
   Hecen on Wanikiya,
   Ohinni niyuhapi.
   Ohinni mayaduha,
   Ohinni cihduzeze,
   Ohinni miyecanpta.
   Wopida eciciye.

3. Wawahtani on nita,
   Wokajuju kin hee;
   Wowaonsida duha,
   Hecen on wacinciye;
   Woniya Wakan kin he
   On mayaduteca kte,
   On mayaduwakan kte,
   He ionsimada ye.

WORDS: *Dakota Odowan: Dakota Hymns*

Jesus Loves Me

1. Je-sus loves me! This I know, for the Bi-ble tells me so.
2. Je-sus loves me! This I know, as he loved so long a-go,
3. Je-sus loves me still to-day, walk-ing with me on the way,

Lit-tle ones to him be-long; they are weak, but he is strong.
tak-ing chil-dren on his knee, say-ing, "Let them come to me."
want-ing as a friend to give light and love to all who live.

Refrain

Yes, Je-sus loves me! Yes, Je-sus loves me!

Yes, Je-sus loves me! The Bi-ble tells me so.

WORDS: St. 1 Anna B. Warner; sts. 2-3 David Rutherford McGuire
MUSIC: William B. Bradbury

Cherokee

Cherokee:

1. Tsisa a ki ke yu ha
   Koh wel a khi no hih se
   Tsu nah sti ka Tsu tse li
   u hli ni ki tih ye hno

Refrain

Tsis a ki ke yu
Tsis a ki ke yu
Tsis a ki ke yu
a khi no hih se ho.

Phonetic transliteration:

1. Jee-suh gee gey yoo hee
   Go wehl ah kee no hee seh
   Joo nah stee kah joo jeh lee
   Oo hlee nee kee dee yeh no.

Refrain

Jee-suh gee gay yoo,
Jee-suh gee gay yoo,
Jee-suh gee gay yoo,
Ah gee no hee seh no.

WORDS: Cherokee transcription by Robert Bushyhead; common phonetic transliteration by Jennie Lee Fife (Cherokee) © 1992
Cherokee transcription © 1989 The United Methodist Publishing House

Muscogee (Creek)

Muscogee (Creek):

1. Cesvs vc vnokeces
   Cokv-rakkot cv kices.
   Hopuetvke enaket's;
   Yekcvkekis, ent yekes.

Refrain

Vc vnokeces,
Vc vnokeces,
Vc vnokeces,
Nakcokvt cv kices.

Phonetic transliteration:

1. Chee-suhs ahj-ah-no-kee-chees
   Cho-kah-thah-ko chah-kay-chees.
   Ho-pwee-tah-kee ee-nah-kehts;
   Yeek-chah-kay-kees, en yeek-chees.

Refrain

Ahj ah-no-kee-chees,
Ahj ah-no-kee-chees,
Ahj ah-no-kee-chees,
Nahk-cho-kuht chah kay-chees.

WORDS: Trad. Muscogee text; anon. phonetic transliteration with corrections by Leona Sullivan (Creek)

Jesus Our Friend and Brother

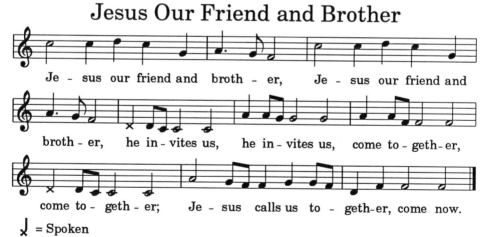

♩ = Spoken

WORDS: Attr. to Ova'hehe; translation by David Graber and others
MUSIC: Attr. to Ova'hehe; transcription by David Graber
Translation and music transcription © 1982 Mennonite Leaders' Council

Kiowa Hymn 29

♩ = 72

Daw-k'yah-ee   gaw-thah-ee-do   aym-o-thah-daw - pay.

Daw-k'yah-ee   gaw-thah-ee-do, gaw-thah-ee-do,   aym o-daw pay

gaw-thah-ee do - do.   Daw - k'yah - ee

gaw-thah-ee do   aym-o - thah-daw - pay.   pay.

Kiowa:

Daw-k'yah-ee gaw-thahy-dow
aym-owthah-dawpay.
Daw-k'yah-ee gaw-thahy-dow,
gaw-thahy-dow, aym-ow-dawpay
gaw-thahy-dow-dow.
Daw-k'yah-ee gaw-thahy-dow
aym-owthah-dawpay.
Daw-k'yah-ee gaw-thahy-dow,
gaw-thahy-dow, aym-ow-dawpay
gaw-thahy-dow-dow.
Daw-k'yah-ee gaw-thahy-dow
aym-owthah-dawpay.

English paraphrase:

The Son of God is with you, be happy.
The Son of God is with you: he is
with you. You be happy for he is
with you.
The Son of God is with you, be happy.

WORDS: *Kawy-dawkhyah Dawgyah* (*Kiowa Christian Songs*), Hymn 29; common phonetic transliteration by
Marilyn M. Hofstra (Choctaw, Chickasaw) © 1992; Eng. paraphrase by Mike Gallagher and others
MUSIC: Trad. Kiowa; transcription by Marilyn M. Hofstra (Choctaw, Chickasaw) © 1992

Kiowa Prayer Song

♩ = 40

1. Daw - k'yah-ee   ah - dawt - sah - ee   ahn,
2. Daw - k'yah-ee   ah - dawt - sah - ee   ahn,

Daw - k'yah-ee   ah   dawt   sah - ee   ahn,
Daw - k'yah-ee   ah   dawt   sah - ee   ahn,

Ahm   do   gyah - daw   do   ahn,
Ahm   khee - dah - day,   do   ahn

Ah - tsahn   do   gyaht - t'ah - awm.
Ah - tsahn   do   gyaht - t'ah - awm.

Also known and used as a Call to Worship

Kiowa:

1. Daw-k'yah-ee, ah-dawtsahy-ahn,
Daw-k'yah-ee, ah-dawtsahy-ahn.
Ahm dow gyah-daw dow ahn,
Ah-tsahn dow gyaht-t'ah-awm.

2. Daw-k'yah-ee, ah-dawtsahy-ahn,
Daw-k'yah-ee, ah-dawtsahy-ahn.
Ahm khee-dah-day, dow ahn,
Ah-tsahn dow gyaht-t'ah-awm.

English paraphrase:

1. Jesus, Son of God, we come to you
to pray. Jesus, Son of God, we
come to you to pray. To your house
of worship we come in this time of
need; we come to you, help us.

2. Jesus, Son of God, we come to you
to pray. Jesus, Son of God, we
come to you to pray. We come to
pray because it is your day; we
come to you, help us.

WORDS: Trad. Kiowa; common phonetic transliteration by Marilyn M. Hofstra (Choctaw, Chickasaw)
© 1992; Eng. paraphrase by Dorothy Gray (Kiowa) © 1992
MUSIC: Trad. Kiowa; transcription by Marilyn M. Hofstra (Choctaw, Chickasaw) © 1992

Muscogee Hymn 179: Lord Dismiss Us

♩ = 35

1. Chee mee - go - sah - pee-yah-tee Chee mee - go -
2. Mo - mehn yah - mah ee- gah-nah Mo - mehn yah -

sah - pee-yah-tee Chee mee - go - sah - pee-yah-tee Mo-moo-sehn
mah ee- gah-nah Mo- mehn-yah - mah ee- gah-nah En kah-pah -

tehm ah - wah-ehs; Chen helth-gee - tahn po-wah - lahs;
kah - kee - yo-faht, Chen lay - kee - tahn thlo-thlay-cheht,

Chen helth-gee - tahn po-wah - lahs; Chen helth-gee tahn
Chen lay - kee - tahn thlo-thlay-cheht;Chen lay - kee - tahn

po - wah - lahs Mo-meht see - po - wah - hee - chahs.
thlo - thlay-cheht Fee-kah - pee - tahn po yah - chehs.

Muscogee (Creek):

1. Ce mekusapeyvte
Momusen tem vwahes;
Cen herketvn pu'wahlvs;
Mohmet 'sepu'wahecvs.

2. Mohmem yvmv ekvnv
En kvpvkakeyofvt,
Cen liketvn 'roricet.
Fekvpetvn pu 'yaces.

English paraphrase:

1. We pray to you now as we
prepare to dismiss. Share
your peace with us and
dismiss us.

2. Now when we depart from
this earth and arrive at your
dwelling place, we want to rest.

See also "Praise God, from Whom All Blessings Flow"

WORDS: *Muskokee Hymns,* Hymn 179; common phonetic transliteration by Marilyn M. Hofstra (Choctaw, Chickasaw) © 1992; Eng. paraphrase by Leona Sullivan (Creek) © 1992
MUSIC: Trad. Muscogee (Creek); transcription by Marilyn M. Hofstra (Choctaw, Chickasaw) © 1992

One Drop of Blood

WORDS: Trad. Cherokee; common phonetic transliteration by Marilyn M. Hofstra (Choctaw, Chickasaw) © 1992; Eng. paraphrase by Jennie Lee Fife (Cherokee) © 1992

MUSIC: Trad. Cherokee; transcription and harm. by Marilyn M. Hofstra (Choctaw, Chickasaw) © 1992

English paraphrase:

> Our heavenly Father, what do I have to do for you to save me?
> It only takes one drop of blood to wash away our sins.

Refrain

> You are King of Kings,
> the Creator of all things.

Ponca Hymn

Ponca:

Wah-kahn-dah lah-oo-dah-ney
Wah-kahn-dah lah-oo-dah-ney gah
Wee-blah-hah, mah-blee.

Refrain

Weh-kahn-dah lah-oo-dah-ney
Weh-kahn-dah lah-oo-dah-ney
Weh-kahn-dah lah-oo-dah-ney
Weh-kahn-dah lah-oo-dah-ney
Weh-kahn-dah lah-oo-dah-ney gah
Wee-blah-hah, mah-blee.

English translation:

God, he is good;
what God makes is good;
thank you, heavenly Father.

Refrain

God, he is good;
God, he is good;
God, he is good;
God, he is good;
what God makes is good;
thank you, heavenly Father.

WORDS: Trad. Ponca; common phonetic transliteration and Eng. translation by Jim Duncan (Shawnee)
    © 1992
MUSIC: Trad. Ponca; transcription by Marilyn M. Hofstra (Choctaw, Chickasaw) © 1992

Praise God, from Whom All Blessings Flow

Praise God, from whom all bless - ings flow; praise him, all crea - tures here be - low; praise him a - bove, ye heaven - ly host; praise Fa - ther, Son, and Ho - ly Ghost. A - men.

WORDS: Thomas Ken
MUSIC: Attr. to Louis Bourgeois

Cherokee

Oo ne la nuh hi i-ki-do-dah,
Oo ne la nuh hi Oo we-ji,
Oo ne la nuh hi ah-dah-nuh-do,
Keh-di-luh-gwo-dah hna-gwa-se.

WORDS: Trad. Cherokee

Chippewa (Ojibway)

Mah moo yuh wuh mah dah mah buh
Wain je shuh wain dah go ze yung;
Wa yoo se mind Wa gwe se mind,
Kuh ya Pah ne zid O je chog!

WORDS: Trad. Chippewa (Ojibway)

Choctaw

Iki Chihowa fehna ka,
Ushi Chisus aiena ka,
Shilombish Holitopa ma,
Iloh aiokpahanchashke.

WORDS: *Choctaw Hymn Book*, Doxology No. 1

Mohawk

Ron we senna iens ne niio
Ron wa senna iens ne non kwe
Ro wa sen na iens ne ne ken
Ro wasen na iens ro ni ha.

WORDS: Trad. Mohawk

Muscogee (Creek)

Ce Mekusapeyvte
Momusen tem vwahes;
Cen herketvn pu'wahlvs;
Mohmet 'sepu'wahecvs.

WORDS: *Muskokee Hymns*, Hymn 179, stanza 1

Seneca Hymn 152

♩ = 45

1. Do-gas ho - nee-da-o Je-sus ho-wahnt-hon - dey;
2. Hey-nee wahk-nee go-ee yu Ah-gey-ga ney Je - sus
3. Ney-huh nahk-nee go-a-wa, Gao-yah-geh hey gee-dee-oh;

Gao-yah-gey-gwah wah-o-ney-no-on dee-eh:
Nahaht-gwa-sah na-wah-gee-ah dah-gey hah:
Wahey-ahn-dey-ey, kuh ney Chah gao-hey duhs

I - tee-o - wee-no-gweh, Hey-nee-o-nee-go-ee-yu
Shah-gee-wah-gwehn-nee-uhs, O-nee-go-ee-yus-dey-ey
Nah-deeo-yah-gey-o-no, Neh-deyt-ha-see-dah-gey-o

Ney wah-ey jah-go-daht-hey-wah - do.
O-gee-ah-do-want-ah-gehn-neeah-sah-gehn.
Deys-ho-wah-a-sao-nee-o, hodah-nee da-o.

WORDS: *The Seneca Hymnal*, Hymn 152; common phonetic transliteration by Marilyn M. Hofstra (Choctaw, Chickasaw) © 1992; Eng. translation by Alberta Austin (Seneca) © 1992
MUSIC: Wyeth's *Repository of Sacred Music, Part Second*; adapt. by Jim Towry © 1992

Seneca:

1. Do gas' 'ho'ni da oh
   Jesus ho want'hon deh;
   Gao'yah ge'gwa wa'one noon'
      'dyieh;
   Eye tio wi'no'gweh,
   He ni oh'ni goi'yuh
   Neh wa'eh jago'dat he'wah doh.

2. He'ni wak'ni goi'yu
   A ge'ga ne Jesus
   Naat gwah'sah nawa'gyah da'ge hah
   Shah gi'wa gwen ni'yus,
   Ohni go'iyus deeh
   O gyah'do want a gen'nyah sah geh.

3. Neh huh' nakni'goa wah,
   Gao'yah gen he gih'dyoh
   Wae yan deeh, kuh, ne Cha gao'he
      dus
   Na dio yah'ge'o noh,
   Neh det ha'sih da'geoh,
   Des ho waah'sao nyoh', ho'da ni
      daoh.

English translation:

1. It's true they are blessed;
   we who listen to Jesus;
   those who are going toward heaven;
   we will tell the people,
   how happy his mind is
   when we repented.

2. How peaceful my mind is.
   I have seen Jesus;
   his blood it will help me.
   When I first came to believe
   it gave me peace of mind.
   I have received it into my heart.

3. That's how my mind has become.
   In heaven I will live there.
   I came to know Jesus too.
   People of the heaven,
   there at his feet,
   they are praising him.
   He is blessed.

Seneca Hymn 193

1. Je-sus ney Sho-gwah wehn nee-yuh, Gao-yah-geh-tha-deeo:
2. Yo-an-jah-geh ney-huh heys-gwah Gao-yah-geh-tha-deeo:
3. Heys-ga-gont dant-hey ney Je-sus, Gao-yah-geh-tha-deeo:

Ah-so ney-huh sho-gwah ho-o gwah, Gao-yah-gey-tha-deeo.
Tsho-gwa-nok-hey hey-o-yo-no Gao-yah-gey-tha-deeo.
O-nah-da-sho gwah-yah-do-weht Gao-yah-gey-tha-deeo.

Refrain

Ga-o dah-sweht, swi wah-nev-ah-go,

Shee-swi-wah-gwehn-nee-yuhs Gao-yah-gey-tha-deeo.

Seneca:

1. Jesus neh Sho gwa'wen ni yuh,
   Gao'yah geh thah dyoh:
   Ah'soh neh'huh sho'gwa nooh gwah,
   Gao'yah geh thah dyoh.

   Refrain

   Ga oh'da swet, swai'wa neh'a goh,
   She swai'wa gwen ni yus
   Gao' yah geh thah dyoh.

English translation:

1. Jesus is our Lord and Savior,
   in heaven he lives there.
   He still loves us,
   in heaven he lives there.

   Refrain

   You all come this way, you sinners.
   You all believe in him again,
   in heaven he lives there.

WORDS: *The Seneca Hymnal*, Hymn 193; common phonetic transliteration by Marilyn M. Hofstra (Choctaw, Chickasaw) © 1992; Eng. translation by Alberta Austin (Seneca) © 1992
MUSIC: Trad. Seneca; transcription by Jim Towry © 1992

2. Yo an'jah geh neh huh' hehsgwah
Gao' yah get that dyoh.
Tsho gwa'nok eh he o'yo'noh
Gao' yah geh thah dyoh.

3. Hes ga gont' dant eh' neh Jesus,
Gao'yah geh thah dyoh.
Onah' da sho'gwa yah'do wet
Gao'yah geh thah dyoh.

2. On the earth he was there,
in heaven he lives there.
He came back after us,
in heaven he lives there.

3. Once more Jesus will come back,
in heaven he lives there.
Now he will judge us,
in heaven he lives there.

Song of Thanksgiving

♩ = 70

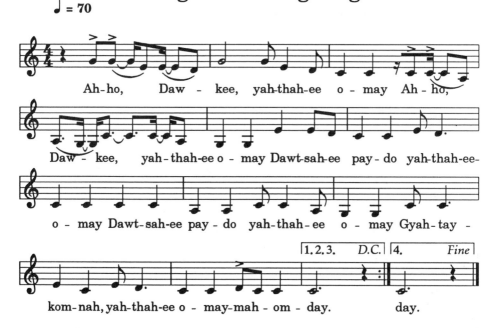

Ah-ho, Daw - kee, yah-thah-ee o - may Ah - ho,

Daw - kee, yah-thah-ee o - may Dawt-sah-ee pay - do yah-thah-ee-

o - may Dawt-sah-ee pay - do yah-thah-ee o - may Gyah-tay -

1. 2. 3.   D.C. | 4.   Fine

kom-nah, yah-thah-ee o - may-mah - om - day.   day.

"This is a Kiowa hymn that my grandfather Edgar Keahbone would sing as he started from the door of the church and walked toward the altar. We were taught that God is with us—look to Him and He will grant you the petition that is in your heart.

We were also taught the Kiowa way. Our elders say to sing this song four times because ... the sun comes up in the East, the sun sets in the West, the wind blows from the South, and the wind blows from the North."   —Trina Lue Stumblingbear

Kiowa:

Ah ho dau kei yah tai ohm mai
Ah ho dau kei yah tai ohm mai
Dau chai pado yahn tai ohm mai
Geah tape kom na yahn tai ohm
Mai mah ohm dai.

English paraphrase:

Thank you, God, for your help.
Thank you, God, for your help.
It was through prayers that I received
your help.
I cried out in desperation and you
have helped me.
I am so happy and thankful.

WORDS: Native text by Edgar Keahbone (Kiowa); common phonetic transliteration by Marilyn M. Hofstra (Choctaw, Chickasaw) © 1992; Eng. paraphrase by Edgar Keahbone (Kiowa). Native text and Eng. paraphrase © 1991 by Trina Lue Stumblingbear

MUSIC: Edgar Keahbone (Kiowa); transcription by Marilyn M. Hofstra (Choctaw, Chickasaw) © 1992

Sweet By and By

1. There's a land that is fair - er than day, and by
2. We shall sing on that beau - ti - ful shore the mel-
3. To our boun - ti - ful Fa - ther a - bove, we will

faith we can see it a - far; for the Fa - ther waits
o - di - ous songs of the blest, and our spir - its shall
of - fer our trib - ute of praise, for the glo - ri - ous

o - ver the way, to pre-pare us a dwell-ing place there.
sor-row no more, not a sigh for the bless-ing of rest.
gift of his love, and the bless-ings that hal - low our days.

Refrain

In the sweet by and by,
In the sweet by and by, by and by,

We shall meet on that beau - ti - ful shore; by and by,

WORDS: S. F. Bennett
MUSIC: J. P. Webster

In the sweet by and by,
In the sweet by and by, by and by,
we shall meet on that beau - ti - ful shore.

Muscogee (Creek)

Muscogee (Creek):

1. Ekuvnv herusat ocet os;
   Nettv sen hvyayvket omes.
   Vkvsvmkv eteropotten,
   Hopvyis, heceye tetayes.

Refrain

   Oketv cvmpusan
   Mv tvpalv mimv herusan,
   Oketv cvmpusan
   Mv tvpalvn teheceyvres.

2. Afvcakat en yvhiketvn
   Mv tvpalvn yvhikeyvres;
   "Stofis pu feknokhokakares;
   Yuksv-sekon fekapeyvres.

3. Purke merkv es fvcke likat
   Pum vkvsvmkvn emeyres;
   Heren epu 'nokecvtet ok'
   Mont em merkv oce munkvt ok'.

Phonetic transliteration:

1. Ee-kuh-nah hee-thloo-saht o-cheet
   os;
   Nit-tuh sen huh-yuh-yah-kit o-miss,
   Uh-kuh-sum-kuh ee-tee-thlo-pote-ten,
   Ho-poo-yes, hee-chee-yee tee-tah-yis.

Refrain

   O-kee-tah chum-poo-sahn
   Muh tuh-pah-luh may-muh hee-thloo-
   sahn,
   O-kee-tah chum-poo-sahn
   Muh tuh-pah-lun tee-hee-chee-yuh-
   thleeze.

2. Ah fuch-kah-kut in yuh-hay-kee-ton
   Muh tuh-pah-lun yuh-hay-kee-yuh-
   thleeze;
   "Sto-fes poo feek-nok-ho-kee-kah-
   thleeze;
   Yok-sah-see-kon fee-kuh-pee-yah
   thleeze.

3. Pulth-ke milth-kuh es fuch-kee lay-
   kaht
   Pum uh-kuh-sum-kon ee-mee-yuh-
   thleeze;
   He-thlen ee-po no-kee-chuh-tet-ok;
   Mont em milth-kuh o-chee mon-kut
   ok.

WORDS: Trad. Muscogee text; common phonetic transliteration by Leona Sullivan (Creek) © 1992

'Twas in the Moon of Wintertime

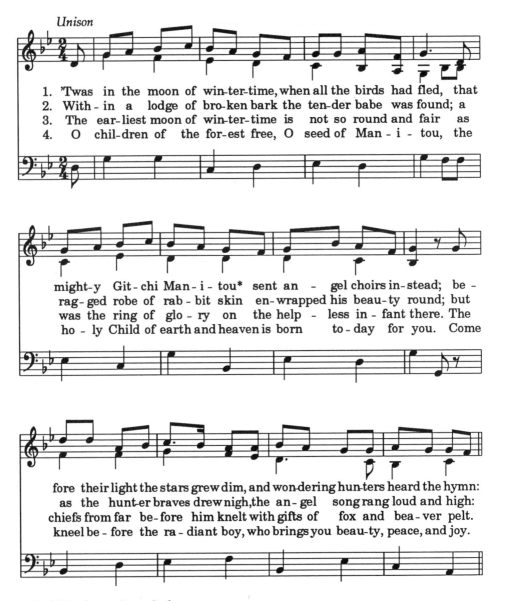

Unison

1. 'Twas in the moon of win-ter-time, when all the birds had fled, that
2. With-in a lodge of bro-ken bark the ten-der babe was found; a
3. The ear-liest moon of win-ter-time is not so round and fair as
4. O chil-dren of the for-est free, O seed of Man-i-tou, the

might-y Git-chi Man-i-tou* sent an - gel choirs in-stead; be -
rag-ged robe of rab-bit skin en-wrapped his beau-ty round; but
was the ring of glo-ry on the help - less in-fant there. The
ho-ly Child of earth and heaven is born to-day for you. Come

fore their light the stars grew dim, and won-dering hun-ters heard the hymn:
as the hunt-er braves drew nigh, the an-gel song rang loud and high:
chiefs from far be-fore him knelt with gifts of fox and bea-ver pelt.
kneel be-fore the ra-diant boy, who brings you beau-ty, peace, and joy.

* Gitchi Manitou = Great God

WORDS: Trad. Huron by Jean de Brebeuf; Eng. paraphrase by Jesse Edgar Middleton
MUSIC: French Canadian melody
Eng. text used by permission of Frederick Harris Music Co. Limited, Canada

Refrain

Je-sus your King is born, Je - sus is born, in ex-cel-sis glo - ri - a.

Huron:

Esteiaron de tsonoue, Jesous ahatonhia.
Onna-ouate oua d'oki n'ou ouanda skoua en tak.
En nonchien skouatchi hotak, n'on ouandi lonra chata,
Jesous ahatonhia, Jesous ahatonhia, Jesous ahatonhia.

What a Friend We Have in Jesus

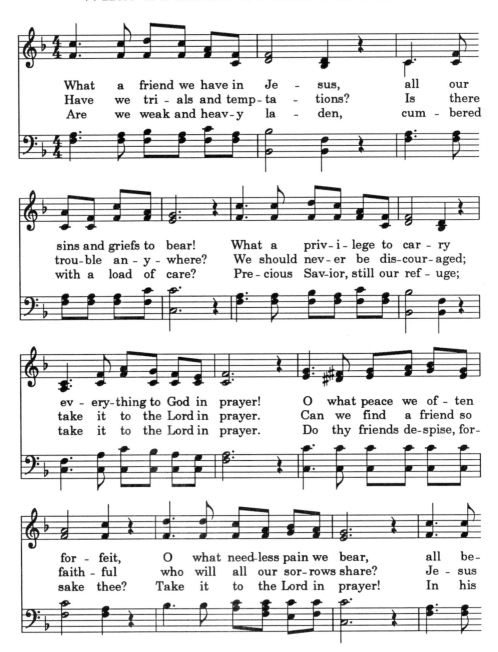

What   a friend we have in   Je - sus,   all   our
Have   we tri - als and temp - ta - tions?   Is   there
Are   we weak and heav - y   la - den,   cum - bered

sins and griefs to bear!   What a   priv - i - lege to car - ry
trou - ble an - y - where?   We should nev - er be dis-cour-aged;
with a load of care?   Pre - cious Sav-ior, still our ref - uge;

ev - ery-thing to God in prayer!   O what peace we of - ten
take it to the Lord in prayer.   Can we find a friend so
take it to the Lord in prayer.   Do thy friends de-spise, for-

for - feit,   O   what need-less pain we bear,   all be-
faith - ful   who will all our sor-rows share?   Je - sus
sake thee?   Take it   to the Lord in prayer!   In his

WORDS: Joseph M. Scriven
MUSIC: Charles C. Converse

cause we do not car - ry   ev - ery-thing to God in prayer.
knows our ev - ery weak-ness;   take it to the Lord in prayer.
arms he'll take and shield thee;   thou wilt find a sol-ace there.

Seneca

Seneca:

Ga-o' da-swe-t, i-s ne jo-gweh,
I-s ne swai-wane'agoh;
Ga-o' da-swe-t, he niga-ye';
Nodanideo-sha' Jesus.
Hodehsa'oh, hodehsa'oh,
Ne' ejiswaya'dagwat;
Ga-o' da-swe-t, i-s ne jo-gweh,
I-s, ne swai-wane'agoh.

English paraphrase:

This way you all come;
you the people are all sinners.
Where lays his spirit, he is ready,
he will take you.

Can also be sung to "Farther Along" and "Face to Face"

WORDS: Trad. Seneca text; anon. Eng. paraphrase

CR SHAW

Worship Resources

Through the years

*they developed traditions
that kept them strong
so they passed them on to their children
and it kept them strong.*

<u>Calls to Worship</u>

Be with Us, Great Spirit

Leader: We are your children.

People: **We have heard you in the winds, seen you in the sunrise; we have felt your kindness in the seasons.**

Leader: Great Spirit, we know you! We hear you speak!

People: **We know this very moment you are near to us as the air surrounds us and fills our lungs with life.**

Leader: Be with us, Great Spirit. Show us the way you would have us go!

From *Family Prayer* by Sister Kevin Marie Flynn. Used by permission.

Christ Is the Center

Leader I: We will act out the ceremonial, recalling that Christ is the center of creation, the central reality of God's plan for the world, the central reality of our lives as Christians. As we face each of the four directions, we will respond in prayer. Following each prayer, we will return to face the center, reminded each time that it is Christ who is able to bring healing and salvation and who by his Spirit is able to renew the face of the earth.

Leader II: First, let us all face a center point. *(all face center, pause)*

Leader I: From the East, the direction of the rising sun, come wisdom and knowledge.

Leader II: Let us face East *(all face East, pause)* and let us pray:

All: **Enable us, O God, to be wise in our use of the resources of the earth, sharing them in justice, partaking of them in thankfulness.** *(all face center, pause)*

Leader II: From the South comes guidance, and the beginning and end of life.

Leader I: Let us face South *(all face South, pause)* and let us pray:

All: **May we walk good paths, O God, living on this earth as sisters and brothers should, rejoicing in one another's blessings, sympathizing in one another's sorrows, and together with you renewing the face of the earth.** *(all face center, pause)*

Leader II: From the West come purifying waters.

Leader I: Let us now face West *(all face West, pause)* and pray that the Spirit of God may again breathe over the waters making them pure, making them fruitful. Let us pray:

All: **We pray that we too may be purified so that life may be sustained and nurtured over the entire face of the earth.** *(all face center, pause)*

Leader II: From the North come purifying winds. O God, you have been called breath and wind of life.

Leader I: Let us face North *(all face North, pause)* and let us pray:

All: **May the air we breathe be purified so that life may be sustained and nurtured over the entire face of the earth.** *(all face center, pause)*

From Lakota prayer tradition by Christian Native American Women for World Day of Prayer 1981. © 1981 Church Women United.

Embrace and Celebrate the Sacred Circle of Life

Leader: We come together today to celebrate the contributions Native People of this land have made to God's Church.

People: **We learn from them, that life is a sacred circle, of which there is no beginning and no end.**

Leader: We are all a part of that circle, ever contributing, ever receiving.

People: **Native Americans teach us that as a part of the circle, we must care for all of God's creation.**

Leader: We know that God's creation includes all that is a part of this earth: the wingeds, the two-leggeds, plants, and the sky.

People: **We remember and worship God the Creator throughout our daily lives, even as we look at a tree, the grass, or the sky.**

Leader: For Genesis reminds us that God looked at everything and was very pleased.

All: **We join in this Native American Awareness Sunday, remembering that worship encompasses all of life. We embrace and celebrate the sacred circle of life!**

Cynthia Abrams (Seneca) © 1989

Respect for All of Life

Leader: Thank you, Lord, for the people gathered around us today. Let us take this time to give thanks for these things of the earth that give us the means of life.

People: **Thank you for the plants, animals, and birds that we use as food and medicine.**

Leader: Thank you for the natural world in which we find the means to be clothed and housed.

People: **Thank you, Lord, for the ability to use these gifts of the natural world.**

Leader: Help us to see our place among these gifts; not to squander them or think of them as means for selfish gain.

People: **May we respect the life of all you have made.**

All: **May our spirits be strengthened by using only what we need and may we use our strength to help those who need us.**

From Mohawk prayer tradition, by Sue Ellen Herne (Mohawk) © 1992

Share the Creator's Gifts

Leader: We believe that the Creator made all people to be spiritual.

People: **And that to live as the Creator intended we must work with our God.**

Leader: Live by spiritual truths; show good example for your brothers and sisters.

People: **But most of all, share the Creator's gifts in gratitude.**

From *Vision on the Wind* by Larry Mens. Used by permission.

We Are All Related

Leader: We share our stories.

People: Each of us brings a unique story and gifts from the Creator.

Leader: Our stories are about journeys of faith.

People: We walk a path of righteousness.

Leader: We share our path with all creation.

People: We are all related.

From Eastern Cherokee prayer tradition by Z. Susanne Aikman (Eastern Cherokee) © 1992

Prayers of Confession $5/4/03$

Creator, Give Us Hearts to Understand

Creator, give us hearts to understand; never to take from creation's beauty more than we give; never to destroy wantonly for the furtherance of greed; never to deny to give our hands for the building of earth's beauty; never to take from her what we cannot use.

Give us hearts to understand that to destroy earth's music is to create confusion; that to wreck her appearance is to blind us to beauty; that to callously pollute her fragrance is to make a house of stench; that as we care for her she will care for us. Amen.

Christian Native American Women for World Day of Prayer 1981. © 1981 Church Women United.

We Are Forgiven $5/4/03$

Leader: The circle of love is repeatedly broken because of the sin of exclusion. We create separate circles: the inner circle and the outer circle, the circle of power and the circle of despair, the circle of privilege and the circle of deprivation.

People: **Forgive us our sins, as we forgive all who have sinned against us.**

Leader: The circle of love is broken whenever there is alienation, whenever there is misunderstanding, whenever there is insensitivity and a hardening of the heart.

People: **Forgive us our sins, as we forgive all who have sinned against us.**

Leader: The circle of love is broken whenever we cannot see eye to eye, whenever we cannot link hand to hand, whenever we cannot live heart to heart and affirm our differences.

People: **Forgive us our sins, as we forgive all who have sinned against us.**

Leader: Through God's grace we are forgiven, by the mercy of our Creator, through the love of the Christ, and in the power of the Spirit. Let us rejoice and be glad.

All: **Glory to God. Amen.**

From "Circle of Love," *Woman Prayer Woman Song* by Miriam Therese Winter. Adapted by Native American Ministry of Presence, Denver, Colorado.

© 1987 by Medical Mission Sisters. Used by permission.

Other Prayers

All Things Hold Beauty

Thank you, Lord, for all that you have given us.

Thank you for the beauty of the universe that you created; the trees, the sky, the mountains, the rain.

All things hold beauty in themselves and all are related and touch each creature of the earth. You created the rhythm and pattern of the universe in a harmony of movement, sight, and sound.

Help us to appreciate your creation and to live with our eyes, ears, and hearts open to your message. Amen.

From Mohawk prayer tradition by Sue Ellen Herne (Mohawk) © 1991

Around Us It Is Blessed
(Benediction)

Unison

Before us it is blessed.
Behind us it is blessed.
Below us it is blessed.
Above us it is blessed.
Around us it is blessed as we set out with Him.
Our speech is blessed as we set out for Him.
With beauty before me,
    with beauty behind me,
    with beauty below me,
    with beauty above me,
    with beauty around me,
    I set out for a holy place indeed.

From Navajo prayer tradition

Beauty Is Before Me

Now Talking God,
    with your feet I walk.
I walk with your limbs.
I carry forth your body.
For me your mind thinks.
Your voice speaks for me.
Beauty is before me
    and beauty is behind me.

Above and below me hovers the beautiful.
I am surrounded by it.
I am immersed in it.
In my youth I am aware of it.
And in old age
    I shall walk quietly
    the beautiful trail.

From Navajo prayer tradition by Christian Native American Women for World Day of Prayer 1981.
© 1981 Church Women United.

Guide Us to Show Your Love

Leader: Creator, you have given us different shades of skin, color of eyes, and cultural traditions.

People: **We regret stereotypes and past transgressions with sisters and brothers of other races.**

Leader: You have given us a golden rule that too often we don't apply to culture and tradition.

People: **We fail our own beauty when we neglect the graces others offer us.**

All: **Hear our prayers, Lord Jesus, Bringer of Peace to all creation; forgive us when we do not please you and guide us to show your love through our words and deeds.**

From Eastern Cherokee prayer tradition by Z. Susanne Aikman (Eastern Cherokee) © 1992

Help Us to Be Upright

Oh Great Spirit, when we walk the path of beauty with sincerity, honesty, courage, and truthfulness, we are like the upright basket which can hold the fruits of harvest. We can receive and share the blessings abundantly. But when we have strayed from the beauty path and are not trustworthy, honest, or reliable, we are like the basket turned over. We cannot contain, receive, or give of the many blessings of life. When we are upside down we are empty and useless. Help us to always be upright, to receive and share the blessings of life.

Anonymous

In Beauty May I Walk

In beauty may I walk.
All day long may I walk.
Through the returning seasons may I walk. . . .
With beauty may I walk.
With beauty before me, may I walk.
With beauty behind me, may I walk.
With beauty above me, may I walk.
With beauty below me, may I walk.
With beauty all around me, may I walk.
In old age wandering on a trail of beauty, lively, may I walk.
In old age wandering on a trail of beauty, living again, may I walk.
It is finished in beauty.
It is finished in beauty.

Excerpt from "A Prayer ...," *Navaho Myths, Prayers, and Songs with Texts and Translations* by Washington Matthews, University of California Publications in American Archaeology and Ethnology, Volume 5, No. 2 (1907-1910)

My Spirit Is One with You

My spirit is one with you, Great Spirit.

You strengthen me day and night to share my very best with my brothers and sisters.

You, whom my people see in all of creation and in all people, show your love for us.

Help me to know, like the soaring eagle, the heights of knowledge.

From the Four Directions, fill me with the four virtues of fortitude, generosity, respect, and wisdom; so that I will help my people walk in the path of understanding and peace.

From Lakota prayer tradition

A Psalm of the Woodlands

Leader: As a tree in the forest becomes tall reaching for the light,

People: **May we grow above the shadows of sin, fear, and doubt.**

Leader: As it gives shelter and shade to its friends of fur and feather,

People: **So may we help those brothers and sisters that are smaller and weaker than ourselves.**

Leader: The tree sends down roots deep into the soil that it may be nourished by Mother Earth;

People: **May we be as firmly grounded by the love of Christ and sustained by his grace.**

Leader: If a tree falls and decays, it provides nourishment for new plants and gives its place in the sun for others.

People: **Our Lord and Savior died to make new life and a new place for us.**

Leader: When a tree in the forest is cut down, its wood is used for shelter and fuel;

People: **Jesus taught that only when life is surrendered, when love is poured out, can we build his kingdom and reflect the warmth of his spirit.**

Milton Vahey © 1992

Shawnee Marriage Prayer

Now for you the North wind does not blow;
you are shelter to one another.

Now for you there is no hunger;
each brings what the other needs.

Now for you there is no darkness;
you have learned to see with the heart.

Now for you there is no loneliness;
two have become one.

From Shawnee prayer tradition by Fred A. Shaw (Shawnee Nation U.R.B.) © 1990

We Are God's Essence
(Benediction)   5/4/03

Leader: God is before us.

People: **God is behind us.**

Leader: God is above us.

People: **God is below us.**

Leader: God's words shall come from our mouths.

People: **For we are all God's essence, a sign of God's love.**

Leader: All is finished in beauty.

All: **All is finished in beauty.**

From Navajo prayer tradition

We Pray for Your Wisdom

Leader: Great Spirit, whose dry lands thirst, help us to find the way to refresh your lands.

People: **We pray for your power to refresh your lands.**

Leader: Great Spirit, whose waters are choked with debris and pollution, help us to find the way to cleanse your waters.

People: **We pray for your knowledge to find the way to cleanse the waters.**

Leader: Great Spirit, whose beautiful earth grows ugly with misuse, help us to find the way to restore the beauty of your handiwork.

People: **We pray for your strength to restore the beauty of your handiwork.**

Leader: Great Spirit, whose creatures are being destroyed, help us find the way to replenish them.

People: **We pray for your power to replenish the earth.**

Leader: Great Spirit, whose gifts to us are being lost in selfishness and corruption, help us to find the way to restore our humanity.

All: **We pray for your wisdom to find the way to restore our humanity.**

Christian Native American Women for World Day of Prayer 1981.
© 1981 Church Women United

We Thank You, Great Spirit
(Litany of Thanksgiving)

Leader: For life, and the gift of living each day,

People: **We thank you, Great Spirit.**

Leader: For calling us to be Christians by our baptism,

People: **We thank you, Great Spirit.**

Leader: For our family and friends,

People: **We thank you, Great Spirit.**

Leader: For the great gift of Mother Earth,

People: **We thank you, Great Spirit.**

Leader: For the sun that rises in the East to give us warmth and light
            and for its brilliance as it sets in the West,

People: **We thank you, Great Spirit.**

Leader: For the soft wind and rain that come from the South,

People: **We thank you, Great Spirit.**

Leader: For the shelter you provide to protect us from the North
            winds,

People: **We thank you, Great Spirit.**

Leader: For the flowers that bloom, leaves that change color, great
            bodies of water that surround us, and all animals, great
            and small,

People: **We thank you, Great Spirit.**

Leader: For the gift of vision to see and the gift of voice that we send
            to you in prayer and praise,

People: **We thank you, Great Spirit. Amen.**

From *Family Prayer* by Sister Kevin Marie Flynn. Used by permission.

Other Resources   5/4/03

Blessing of the People
(Opening Ceremony and Closing Prayer)

As the people gather, either sweet grass, cedar, or sage (or all three) can be used as incense and burned in a basin sending forth its fragrance.

Opening Ceremony

Creator, Grandfather, we offer the burning of (sweet grass/cedar/sage) as a purification, a reminder for those gathered here to cleanse our thoughts and hearts that we may hear and be guided by your word and direction.

We thank you for all our relatives: the four-leggeds, the wingeds, the star people of the heavens, and all living things you have blessed us with to sustain this life.

Empower each of us through the bringer of Peace, Jesus Christ, to seek and make change for a better life for all people and all creation.

Hear our prayers this day and everyday. Accept our thanks for all the blessings we enjoy and for those yet to come to us. Aho-Amen.

Closing Prayer

Great Spirit, Creator, behold us! You have placed a great power in the direction from which many generations have come forth and have returned.

The generation that is here today wishes to cleanse and purify itself, that we may live again. May the lingering fragrance of (sweet grass/cedar/sage) purify the feet and hands of the two-leggeds, that we may walk forward upon the sacred earth, raising our faces to the Creator.

Bless our going out from here and each new morning you grant to us; that we will make a difference in this world following the sacred red path marked for us by your Son, the Messenger of Peace and Justice.

Your Spirit, my spirit, may they unite to make one spirit in healing. Aho-Amen.

From Eastern Cherokee prayer tradition by Z. Susanne Aikman (Eastern Cherokee) © 1992

A Blessing of Union

Creator's love for us is unconditional, use it as a model for your love for each other. He does not change us: He allows us to choose to change, then supports us in our decision and throughout the change.

As individuals you are not twins, but mirrors for each other, reflecting your gifts and strengths and complementing the other's weakness. Celebrate your differences!

Like traditional moccasins, you do not become a perfectly matched pair, but two different, equally unique works of art that complement each other's beauty throughout your life.

May the Bringer of Peace, Son of Creator, bless this union and all creation, our relatives, with pure white light and everlasting love.

From Eastern Cherokee prayer tradition by Z. Susanne Aikman (Eastern Cherokee) © 1992

The Jumping Mouse Story

They say that one day the Great Wolf was standing by alone and crying. In his sadness, loneliness, and pain, he had lost his eyes and was blind. And as the Great Wolf stood there crying, his Little Mouse brother came. Little Mouse looked up and felt very sad to see this Great Wolf crying. Little Mouse was very tiny, but asked the Great Wolf, "Why is it that you cry?" And the Great Wolf said, "In my sadness and my loneliness and pain, I have lost my eyes and I am blind."

Without having to think because of his teachings, Little Mouse took his own eyes out and, reaching out, gave them to Great Wolf. Great Wolf took the little mouse eyes and put them in and at once began to feel powerful because he could see again. In fact, he almost forgot his Little Mouse brother standing there blind; but he looked down and said, crying, "Little Mouse, why did you give me your own eyes?"

And Little Mouse said, "I realize before all the universe and before the Great Spirit, I am very humble and I have always been taught to give my very best to my brothers and sisters." Great Wolf began to weep even more for his Little Mouse brother.

In his tears, though, he could still remember a truth. He remembered there was a sacred lake where anyone could make offerings to the Creator, the Four Directions, and Mother Earth. What we ask will come to pass and will come true if only we have the patience to wait.

So he took his Little Mouse brother by the hand, and Great Wolf and Little Mouse began their journey. Among the Lakota people, there are many, many stories about the journey of Great Wolf and Little Mouse looking for the Sacred Lake.

Finally one day when it seemed that they could not go another step, when they had been through many sufferings and problems, they came to the top of a mountain and Great Wolf looked over and down below and saw the most beautiful lake he had ever seen. He looked at the beautiful lake and said, "Oh, Little Mouse, if you could only see the beauty of the lake below us. We have finally come to the end of our journey."

And he took Little Mouse brother by the hand, and they walked down to the edge of the lake. There Great Wolf called upon the powers of the universe, upon the Eagle People, upon the Hawk People, and the Thunderbird People, and offered the tobacco to all the powers of the sky, and called upon the power of the West, from which come darkness and other powers; of the North, from which come the white snows; of the East, from which comes the red sunrise; and the South, where the yellow deserts lie. He called to the Creator of all good things. He called upon the powers of Mother Earth to help his Little Mouse brother. Then he said to Little Mouse, "The Creator, the Great Spirit, speaks to each one of us in our own way and in our own time. Now I am going to leave you alone." So they hugged each other, and they cried because they knew they would not see each other for a while.

Great Wolf left. Little Mouse stood by the edge of the lake, and all of a sudden Little Mouse heard a voice. "Little Mouse brother, jump." So he jumped. "Jump higher." He jumped higher. "Jump higher." And he jumped higher. "JUMP HIGHER." And he jumped higher until Little Mouse felt he was floating in the air.

The voice then said, "Little Mouse brother, because you gave your very best to your brothers and sisters, because you humbled yourself before all creation, from now and forevermore you will be the Great Eagle that will fly high above the people."

From Lakota tradition

Mitakuye Oyasin
All My Relatives

Mitakuye Oyasin (Me-tah-ku-yee O-yah-sin) is a saying that enriches the church as a gift from the spiritual insight and tradition of the Lakota people. It is a marvelously brief but deep expression of what life is. In a few short words, it includes everything spiritual and material, everything seen and unseen, everything that is real. It includes God who is the Great Spirit above all and in all. It includes all his spiritual messengers that move between God and humanity. It includes all the "ancient ones"—those who have died to us but who are now alive to Him and gathered around Him in joy and peace. It includes all men and women, all children who are now living on the face of the earth. It includes all creatures that fly in the air, walk or crawl on the earth or within the earth, and that swim in the waters. It includes the very earth itself and the air that surrounds it like a beautiful blanket.

"All My Relatives" is a saying that recognizes all creation and the Creator as one great family. It extends kinship to everything "that lives and moves and has its being." Nothing can happen to one part of this creation, therefore, that does not in some small way happen to the rest of creation and its Creator. We are FAMILY whether we realize it at times or not; but the earth always realizes it, and the animals always realize it, and God the Spirit never forgets it. To all of them, our kinsfolk, our family members, we owe our very lives; for they support us and keep us in existence. Everything forms a great web of interdependence, giving daily, even second by second, what is needed to keep everything alive. The spider-web can serve as a parable for our minds to dwell on, as to what this family can be likened. Everything is interwoven and interdependent. If one part is unraveling, then it begins to weaken the rest of the web. Conversely, if every part is strong and knows its place and what it is to do, then the entire web is strong and healthy. All creation is one, is harmonious and holy. Like the garment of Jesus, it is a continuous weave and must not be torn apart. Every part needs to be reverenced as holy and worthy of respect so that it can have the freedom to carry out its duties and functions. The earth must not be poisoned and scraped away. The air must not be polluted. The waters must be kept clean. Animals must not be hunted down and killed to extinction. Humanity must be free to praise and glorify God by being alive and healthy, both in body and spirit. God must be free to love and care for us as only he knows how to do. He must be able to love us as a true relative—a Father—Ateunyapi, and we must remove within us whatever it is that keeps that love from flowing into us. . . .

From *Sacred Ground: Reflections on Lakota Spirituality and the Gospel*
© 1986 St. Joseph's Indian School. Used by permission of Tipi Press.

Native American Awareness Sunday

NATIVE AMERICAN
AWARENESS SUNDAY

In creating the design for Native American Awareness Sunday it was important that it be one that all Native Americans could relate to, regardless of the region or culture that they come from. The specific symbols from one Native culture aren't necessarily used in another Native culture. The Iroquois "Tree of Peace" wouldn't necessarily be recognized by the people from the Navajo Nation, for example. I chose to use a symbol that is universal—the sun as light. Light is a generic symbol of awareness. The sun in the design is also below the horizon line. People have varying degrees of awareness of Native American issues, but the issues are there whether they are widely recognized or not, just as the sun is beneath the horizon line whether we see it or not. The sun is a symbol of God in some cultures. In my mind, as I think of the design, humankind is always subject to partial understanding whereas God is the all-encompassing light and truth.

Sue Ellen Herne (Mohawk) © 1992

Parable of the Two Buckets of Water:
The Coming Together of the Old Ways and the New Ways

In the old ways, people make everything they have from what they catch. When the time comes they have a celebration in thanksgiving for what they have. Men talk to young boys; women talk to young girls, to teach them how to live.

The first Christians came. They have teachers. They teach us how to live good, too. The elders and the teachers all teach about God and how to live good. There are no accidents because everybody follows the rules. The buckets are filled. The people all come. Everybody drinks and is filled.

The elders fall silent: The teachers fall silent. Hard times come: Difficulties come. People forget how to live good; accidents happen because people no longer follow the rules. The buckets are empty. All the water goes out. The people are thirsty.

Now the elders are speaking again. The teachers are teaching again. The people are singing again. Now, the people know how to live good. The buckets are filling. The people all come. Everybody drinks and is filled.

From oral tradition in Hooper Bay, Alaska, as told by James Gump (Eskimo).
© 1992 James Gump

Purification and Healing in the Native American Tradition

Ceremonies, rituals, and beliefs vary from one Native American nation to another, often from one Native person to another within the same language group. Some symbols and beliefs, however, are shared by almost all Native peoples. One of these is an understanding of the power of prayer within the sacred circle to purify, cleanse, heal, and renew. I wish to describe two of the rituals and symbols from the Sioux, Ojibway, and other traditions.

Sweat Lodge

Among many of the Plains Indians nations there is a ceremony called the Sweat Lodge or "Inipi" in the Lakota language. This rite is for renewal or spiritual rebirth. In it all four elements—fire, earth, water, and air—contribute to the spiritual, emotional, mental, and physical purification of the participants.

Within a small, dark, dome-shaped lodge of willow saplings and canvas or hides, there is a small pit filled with rocks already heated from a fire outside the lodge. Sage, cedar, and water are sprinkled over these rocks, causing them to give off steam and heat. Black Elk, a Lakota spiritual elder, explains that the lodge itself represents the universe, with the pit at its center as representative of the navel in which the Great Spirit lives with the power of the sacred fire. The willows represent all that grows from Mother Earth. The rocks represent the earth, and also the indestructible and everlasting nature of the Creator. The water reflects values for the people to learn from as it is ever flowing and is a giver of life to everything.

Thomas Goldtooth, a Navajo, explains the symbolism of this ritual in this way: Crawling on hands and knees into the sweat lodge is like "returning to the womb" as an ignorant and pitiful child. The sacred fire heats the rocks, which are the ancient ones, the grandparents who have been here before us and will be here after us. The "living water," when poured over the heated rocks, becomes the "breath of life" that cleanses and makes new. After the prayerful ceremony, one leaves the sweat lodge, leaving behind one's sins and troubles, reentering the world as a new person.

From *Responding with Compassion: Purification and Healing in the American Indian Tradition* by Larry Mens. Used by permission.

Vision Quest

Another life-directing ritual among many Plains Indians nations that can be recreated and used for self-discovery, self-understanding, and healing, is the Vision Quest. Among the Lakota, the ceremony is carried out in the form of a circle and a cross. A person in search of "vision," seeking wisdom and understanding, attempting to reach union with *Wakan-Tanka* (the Great Spirit), fasts and prays for one to four days. This is done under the direction of an elder and follows a prescribed ritual. Upon a hill in a sacred place, the person walks a path to each of the four directions and prays. The person returns to the center between prayers. Through this ritual of prayer and fasting, cleansing and refocusing, one returns from the hill with dreams and images of new directions and new life to share with the elder.

From *Responding with Compassion: Purification and Healing in the American Indian Tradition* by Larry Mens. Used by permission.

Thanksgiving for Water

I want to tell you now about our water—its importance and what it means to us as Yakimas. To the Yakima Nation (located within the state of Washington) water is very important in our daily lives. All through the past generations, our people valued water very much because it meant a way to quench your thirst and a way to keep your body clean. Our foods, the salmon and the wild game, had water to live in and drink and they gave themselves to us so that we were able to feed ourselves. The fish and the deer are very sacred food to us as well as our wild roots, huckleberries, and chokeberries.

Water meant so much to us that we praised it at all times and we gave thanks for it at all times. When we sat down to eat a meal we always had someone pour a little bit of water into the cups and we drank this water before we ate our food. When we finished, again someone poured a little bit of water into our cups, and we completed our meal by drinking this water and giving thanks for our water because it is so important to us.

From Yakima prayer tradition by Elizabeth Henry (Yakima) © 1992

CRSHAW

A Water Ceremony

(from the Caddo tradition)

The water ceremony is done beside a body of water early in the morning as soon as participants awaken. They step into the water (up to the thigh) and face the East and immerse the body (to the neck) up and down in the water four times. Each of the four immersions represents the four directions, the four phases of the moon, the four seasons, and the four phases of human life (infancy, youth, adult, and elder). At the end of the fourth immersion a handful of water is splashed on the face.

Remaining in the water, a morning prayer is then offered: thanks and gratitude for the new day, prayer for constant awareness, and asking for direction on how to be helpful to the creation today. This is a time for remembrance. One is in touch with water from which creation began, in touch with water which surrounded life in the mother's womb, in touch with one's baptism . . . in touch with the Mystery.

Following the time of prayer and moments of quietness, the body is again immersed into the water two more times (the fifth immersion representing the earth, and the sixth, the sky). All six immersions are combined to represent the one Spirit of God, and become part of the great thanksgiving. "Amen" is not said during the ceremony until the end of the day because the whole day becomes a personal prayer. After leaving the water and again facing the East, walk into the day as your prayer and life become one.

The water ceremony can also be used indoors as an early morning event or incorporated into a worship service. If used in the evening, the use of cedar and/or sage can be added. In preparation, water vessels are filled, and a large basin is set on a central table. The basin will be used to catch the water as it is poured over the participants' hands. Also, a small heatproof bowl will be needed to contain the smoldering cedar and/or sage, if it is used. During the early morning event or worship service, participants pass one by one as water is poured (to represent stream movement) from the vessel into the hands and then wiped on the face.

From Caddo tradition by Dayton Edmonds (Caddo). Used by permission.

Indexes

Through my body flows the blood of
singers and dancers,
makers of the dance regalia
carvers and basketmakers,
hunters and fishermen,
all believers in the traditional religion
and the old ways;
I know I am these people
and I have done all those things before
many, many years ago.

Brian D. Tripp (Karuk)

Guide to Pronunciation

Native Americans have various traditions of writing. Similar sounding words are frequently rendered by different combinations of letters. Moreover, different nations and tribes, even different parts of the same tribe, have their own alphabets and/or syllabaries. The purpose of this guide is simply to reflect the standard adopted in this volume for common phonetic spelling (using the Arabic alphabet), and to give users help in pronouncing some of the more difficult vowel and consonantal combinations. The guide was not compiled by professional linguists. Therefore, no claim is implied as to its authority beyond the purposes of this collection.

Vowels and Diphthongs

a	=	as in N**a**vy (Chippewa)
		as in f**a**ther (Dakota, Navajo)
		as in h**a**t, d**a**d, b**a**th (Seneca and others)
aa	=	as in f**a**ther but held for longer duration
ah	=	as in s**a**w, f**a**ll
ai	=	as in **ai**sle (Seneca)
		as in v**ai**n (all others)
au	=	as in la**u**ndry
ay	=	as in d**ay**
e	=	as in m**e**n (Note: In Dakota, **e** is like **a** in place.)
ee	=	as in b**ee**, kn**ee** (Note: In Seneca, **ee** also occurs in combination with other vowels such as **eea** and **eeo**. In these cases, the vowels are elided, not broken into separate syllables.)
eh	=	as in y**e**t, b**e**t, m**e**t
ey	=	as in h**ey**
i	=	as in s**i**t (Navajo)
		as in p**i**ne, s**i**gn (all others)
ii	=	as in s**ee** (Navajo)
o	=	as in g**o**, l**o**w, s**o**
oo	=	as in t**oo**, g**oo**se
u	=	as in **u**nder
uh	=	as in n**u**t, r**u**t, t**u**g
uu	=	as in t**u**be (Inupiaq)

Consonants

ch	=	as in **ch**urch
dl	=	as in i**dl**e
dz	=	as in a**dz**
hlth	=	similar to the consonantal sounds in **health**
g	=	as in **g**o
gw	=	as in **gu**ava
gy	=	as in **gy**necology
ksh	=	similar to the consonantal sounds in **cash**
qw	=	as in **qu**ote
r	=	as in land (Mohawk)
sd	=	as in Tue**sd**ay
sg	=	as in mi**sg**uide
sqw	=	as in **squ**ad
sy	=	as in enun**ci**ate
thl	=	as in a**thl**ete
tl	=	as in grea**tl**y
ts	=	as in lo**ts**
tsh	=	as in ma**tz**o
v	=	as in **ah** (Muscogee, Creek)
wt	=	as in ta**ught**
zh	=	as in plea**s**ure

Diacritical Marks

'	=	marks the accented syllable of a word
_	=	this mark placed underneath a letter gives it a nasal sound similar to that which **n** takes before **g** and **k** in English

Index of Native American Nations and Tribes

Index of Topics and Categories